Discover the
South Central Adirondacks

Four-Season Adventures that Include the
Siamese Ponds Wilderness Area

Discover the
South Central Adirondacks

Four-Season Adventures that Include the Siamese Ponds Wilderness Area

Barbara McMartin

Second Edition

Backcountry Publications
Woodstock, Vermont

An Invitation to the Reader
Over time trails can be rerouted and signs and landmarks altered. If you find that changes have occurred on the routes described in this book, please let us know so that corrections may be made in future editions. The author and publisher also welcome other comments and suggestions. Address all correspondence to:

Editor
Discover the Adirondacks Series
Backcountry Publications
P.O. Box 175
Woodstock, VT 05091

Library of Congress Cataloging-in-Publication Data

McMartin, Barbara.
    Discover the south central Adirondacks: four-season adventures that include the Siamese Ponds Wilderness Area / Barbara McMartin; prepared with the assistance of Dennis Conroy. − 2nd ed.
        p.   cm. − (Discover the Adirondacks series)
    Includes bibliographical references.
    ISBN 0-942440-49-8:
    1. Outdoor recreation−New York (State)−Adirondack Park−Guide
-books. 2. Adirondack Park (N.Y.)−Guide-books. I. Conroy, Dennis. II. Title. III. Series.
GV191.42.N7M36   1990
917.47'5−dc20   89-78462
                                                                        CIP

Published by Backcountry Publications
A division of The Countryman Press, Inc.
Woodstock, Vermont 05091

Printed in the United States of America by McNaughton & Gunn
Typesetting by Sant Bani Press
Series design by Leslie Fry
Layout by Barbara McMartin
Trail overlays by Richard Widhu

Photograph Credits
Barbara McMartin, cover, 2, 10, 18, 29, 33, 41, 44, 49, 52, 62, 70, 74, 77, 84, 93, 95, 98, 102, 107, 120, 129, 134, 139, 141, 143, 144, 152, 154, 156, 164, 172, 182
Edythe Robbins, 6, 174

Photographs
Cover: *Long Pond*
Page 2: *Chimney Mountain*
Page 6: *Peaked Mountain and Pond*
Page 10: *View from Buckhorn Mountain Cliffs*

Acknowledgments

Revisiting favorite destinations is as much fun as discovering new ones. As usual, the walking has been made most pleasant when I have shared it with those who know the area well. This time, walking was especially fun because my husband, W. Alec Reid, was able to accompany me on so many trips. I got to walk all but one of the hikes that others had added to the last revision and I enjoyed what they had discovered.

Don Greene accompanied me on explorations of the upper Kunjamuk. Previous editions have benefited from the work of Dennis Conroy, who walked or skied several trails and wrote about them.

Willard Reed has led coutless expeditions to Chimney Mountain, even enticing me into some of the deepest caves. While his knowledge of the mountain seems encyclopedic, he claims there is still much more to discover. With James C. Dawson, Willard helped me take measurements to refine the map of Chimney. Aerial photographs viewed at APA also helped me draw that map.

Jim Abbott, who has spent several summers as a DEC Wilderness Ranger in the Siamese Ponds Wilderness Area and several winters leading ski trips through it, made several suggestions for this revision.

Patrick Arceri brought me up to date on International Paper Company's policies on the Speculator Tree Farm. Thomas Kapelewski of DEC's Northville Office checked the earlier edition to make sure I was aware of any management changes so I could note them in the revised edition. Also, Margaret Baldwin, DEC Cartographer, kept me apprised of the location of new state acquisitions.

Alec Reid has printed the new photographs for this edition. Stanford Pulrang and Paul Brady joined in accompanying me.

Naturally, this edition was based on the work done for the first, and the assistance of several people remains a vital part of the current edition. Erwin Miller with his knowledge of trails and garnet history, Ted Colwell, William M. White, John Barringer, Ted Abner, Pamela Vogel, Nan Hudnut Clarkson, and William and Lewis Waddell, all contributed valuable background information.

With each guidebook I have written or revised, the circle of friends who have helped me has increased. They have researched walks and historical and geological information, shared their knowledge of the woods, and checked the text for accuracy. I am indebted to all of them for their assistance, but most of all I value their friendship and companionship in exploring the forest we all love.

Contents

Introduction

A REGIONAL GUIDEBOOK ought to tell you enough about an area so that you can enjoy it any time of the year, in many different ways. This guide allows you to discover one part of the vast Adirondack Park: the Siamese Ponds Wilderness Area and the land that surrounds it, from Indian Lake east to the Hudson River and from NY 28 south to NY 8 and 30. This guide also introduces you to the region's history—both natural and social; but it does it in a format that differs from other guides in the *Discover Series* because it describes those histories in the context of a driving trip that circumnavigates the region. Thus the region's historical background is tied to the trailheads and locations you will need to be acquainted with in order to use this guide. For this special introduction, see the second chapter, *Overview.*

How to Use the Discover Guides

The regional guides in the *Discover the Adirondacks* series will acquaint you with each region's access roads and trailheads, its trails and unmarked paths, some bushwhack routes and canoe trips, and its best picnic spots, campsites, and ski-touring routes. At the same time, the guides will introduce you to valleys, mountains, cliffs, scenic views, lakes, streams, and myriad other natural features.

Some of the destinations are within walking distance of the major highways that ring the areas, while others are miles deep into the wilderness. Each description will enable you to determine the best excursion for you to enjoy the natural features you will pass, whether you are on a summer day hike or a winter ski-touring trek. The sections are grouped in chapters according to their access points. Each chapter contains a brief introduction to that area's history and the old settlements and industries that have all but disappeared into the wilderness. Throughout the guide you will find accounts of the geological forces that shaped features of the land, mention of unusual wildflowers, and descriptions of forest stands.

It is our hope that you will find this guide not only an invitation to know and enjoy the woods but a companion for all your adventures there.

MAPS AND NOMENCLATURE

The *Adirondack Atlas*, a map published by City Street Directory of Poughkeepsie, New York, is the best reference for town roads, and has the added advantage of identifying state land. In spite of the fact that it has not been updated to show recent acquisitions, it is a valuable aid where public and private lands are intricately mixed. The new *Adirondack North Country Regional Map* shows all state land including purchases made through 1986. Copies may be obtained free of charge as long as the supply lasts by contacting Adirondack North Country Association, P.O. Box 148, Saranac Avenue, Lake Placid, NY 12946, phone 518-523-9820.

This guide contains maps showing all the routes mentioned and they are adequate for the marked trails. You may still want to carry the USGS (United States Geological Survey) topographic quadrangle sheets for the region, and you ought to have them for the more difficult bushwhacks: Blue Mountain, Indian Lake, Lake Pleasant, Newcomb, Thirteenth Lake, and Harrisburg sheets, all of which are in the 15-minute series.

Maps are available locally in many sporting goods stores. You can order maps from USGS Map Distribution Branch, Box 25286, Denver Federal Center, Denver CO 80225. Maps are more easily obtained from a private source, Timely Discount Topos. You can call them at 1-800-821-7609 to place an order. They will send maps the day after they receive your check or money order. All maps purchased through Timely Discount are on a prepaid basis only; they do not accept credit cards.

DISTANCE AND TIME

Distance along the routes is measured from the USGS survey maps and is accurate to within ten percent. It is given in miles, feet, or yards except where local signs use metric measure. Distance is a variable factor in comparing routes along paths or bushwhacks. Few hikers gauge distance accurately even on well-defined trails.

Time is given as an additional gauge for the length of routes. This provides a better understanding of the difficulty of the terrain, the change of elevation, and the problems of finding a suitable course. Average time for walking trails is 2 miles an hour, 3 miles if the way is level and well-defined; for paths, 1.5–2 miles an hour; and for bushwhacks, 1 mile an hour.

Vertical rise usually refers to the change in elevation along a route up a single hill or mountain; elevation change generally refers to the cumulative change in elevation where a route crosses several hills or mountains.

A line stating distance, time, and vertical rise or elevation change is given with the title of each section describing trails and most paths, but not for less distinct paths and bushwhacks for which such information is too variable to summarize. Distance and times are for *one way only*, unless otherwise stated. The text tells you how to put together several routes into longer treks that will occupy a day or more.

TYPES OF ROUTES

Each section of this guide generally describes a route or a place. Included in the descriptions are such basic information as the suitability for different levels of woods experience, walking (or skiing, paddling, and climbing) times and distances, directions to the access, and, of course, directions along the route itself. The following definitions clarify the terms used in this book.

A route is considered a *trail* if it is so designated by the New York State Department of Environmental Conservation (DEC). This means the trail is routinely cleared by DEC or volunteer groups and adequately marked with official DEC disks. *Blue disks* generally indicate major north-south routes, *red disks* indicate east-west routes, and *yellow disks* indicate the side trails. This scheme is not, however, applied consistently in the Adirondacks.

Some trails have been marked for cross-country skiing, and new *pale yellow disks with a skier* are used. *Large orange disks* indicate *snowmobile* trails, which are limited to Wild Forest Areas. Snowmobiles are permitted on them in winter when there is sufficient snow cover. The guide indicates those trails not heavily used where skiing and snowmobiling may be compatible, but a skier must always be cautious on a snowmobile trail. Hikers can enjoy both ski and snowmobile trails.

A *path* is an informal and unmarked route with a clearly defined foot tread. These traditional routes, worn by fishermen and hunters to favorite spots, are great for hiking. A path, however, is not necessarily kept open, and fallen trees sometimes obliterate its course. The paths that cross wet meadows or open fields often become concealed by lush growth. You should always carry a map and compass when you are following an unmarked path and you should keep track of your location.

There is a safe prescription for walking paths. In a group of three or more hikers, stringing out along a narrow path will permit the leader to scout until the path disappears, at which point at least one member of the party should still be standing on an obvious part of the path. If that hiker remains standing while those in front range out to find the path, the whole group can continue safely after a matter of moments.

Hikers in the north country often use the term *bushwhack* to describe an uncharted and unmarked trip. Sometimes bushwhacking means literally pushing brush aside, but usually it connotes a variety of cross-country walks.

Bushwhacks are an important part of this regional guide because of the shortage of marked trails throughout much of the Adirondack Park and the abundance of little-known and highly desirable destinations for which no visible routes exist. Although experienced bushwhackers may reach these destinations with not much more help than the knowledge of their location, I think most hikers will appreciate these simple descriptions that point out the easiest and most interesting routes. In general, descriptions for bushwhacks are less detailed than those for paths or trails; it is assumed that those who bushwhack have a greater knowledge of the woods than those who walk marked routes.

Bushwhack is defined as any trip through the woods without a trail, a path, or the visible foot tread of other hikers and without markings, signs, or blazes. It also means to make one's way by following a route chosen on a contour map, aided by a compass, using stream beds, valleys, abandoned roads, and obvious ridges as guides. Most bushwhacks require navigating by both contour map and compass, and an understanding of the terrain.

Bushwhack distances are not given in precise tenths of a mile. They are estimates representing the shortest distance one could travel between points. This reinforces the fact that each hiker's cross-country route will be different, yielding different mileages.

A bushwhack is said to be *easy* if the route is along a stream, a lakeshore, a reasonably obvious abandoned roadway, or some similarly well-defined feature. A short route to the summit of a hill or a small mountain can often be easy. A bushwhack is termed *moderate* if a simple route can be defined on a contour map and followed with the aid of a compass. Previous experience is necessary. A bushwhack is rated *difficult* if it entails a complex route, necessitating advanced knowledge of navigation by compass and reading contour maps and land features.

Compass directions for bushwhacks are given in degrees from magnetic north and in degrees from true north. The text will usually specify which reference is used, but if no reference is given, the degrees refer to *magnetic north*.

The guide occasionally describes old *blazed* lines or trails. The word "blaze" comes from the French *blesser* and means to cut or bless. Early loggers and settlers made deep slashes in good-sized trees with an axe to mark property lines and trails. Hunters and fishermen have also often made slashes with knives and though they are not as deep as ax cuts, they too can still be seen. *It is now, and has been for many years, illegal to deface trees in the Forest Preserve in this manner.* Following an old blazed line is challenging but a good way to reach a trailless destination.

You may see *yellow paint daubs on a line of trees* also referred to in the text as *paint blazes*. These lines usually indicate the boundary between private and public lands. Individuals have also used different colors of paint to mark informal routes from time to time. Although it is not legal to mark trails on state land, this guide does refer to such informally marked paths.

All *vehicular traffic*, except snowmobiles on their designated trails, is *prohibited* in the Forest Preserve. Vehicles are allowed on town roads and some roads that pass through state land to reach private inholdings. These roads are described in the guide, and soon the DEC will start marking those old roads that are open to vehicles. Most old roads referred to are town or logging roads that were abandoned when the land around them became part of the Forest Preserve. Now they are routes for hikers, not for vehicles.

There has been an increase in the use of three- and four-wheeled off-road vehicles, even on trails where such use is prohibited. New laws have gone a long way toward stopping this in the Forest Preserve, ensuring that some of the old roads remain attractive hiking routes.

Cables have been placed across many streams by hunters and other sportsmen to help them cross in high water. The legality of this practice has been challenged. Some may be quite safe to use; others are certainly questionable. Using them is not a recommended practice, so when this guide mentions crossing streams to reach some of the hikes, you are urged to do so only when a boat can be used or when you can wade across in low water.

Protecting the Land

Most of the land described in these guides is in the Forest Preserve, lands that have been protected during the past century. No trees may be cut on this state land. All of it is open to the public. The Adirondack Park Agency has responsibility for the Wilderness, Primitive, and Wild Forest guidelines that govern use of the Forest Preserve. Care and custody of these state lands is left to the Department of Environmental Conservation, which is in the process of producing Unit Management Plans for the roughly 130 separate Forest Preserve areas.

A plan for the Siamese Ponds Wilderness, which comprises most of the region covered by this guide, was the first Unit Management Plan (UMP) approved for an Adirondack Wilderness Area. The UMP calls for the marking of several new trails, relocation of camping areas, and the designation of a large area in the southwest corner of the region as a permanently trailless area.

Camping is permitted throughout the public lands except at elevations above 4000 feet and within 150 feet of water and trails. In certain fragile areas, camping is restricted to specific locations, and the state is using a new No Camping disk to mark fragile spots. A few sites within 150 feet of water or trails are marked by Camping disks to indicate camping is permitted. The state-run Indian Lake Island Campsites are assigned and governed by special regulations. You must register at the headquarters off NY 30 by Lewey Lake to use the islands. Otherwise you may camp anywhere without a permit. Permits are needed only for stays that exceed three days or for groups of more than ten campers. Permits can be obtained from the local rangers, who are listed in the area phone books under New York State Department of Environmental Conservation.

Only dead and downed wood may be used for *campfires*. Build fires in designated fire rings or on rock, sand, or gravel, and only when absolutely necessary. Fire is dangerous and can travel rapidly through the duff or organic soil, burning roots and spreading through the forest. Douse fires with water and be sure they are completely out and cold before you leave.

Private lands are generally not open to the public, though some individuals have granted public access across their land to state land. It is always wise to ask before crossing private lands. Be very respectful of private landowners so that public access will continue to be granted. Never enter private lands that have been posted unless you have the owner's permission. Unless the text expressly identifies an area as state-owned Forest Preserve or private land whose owner permits unrestricted public passage, the inclusion of a walk description in this guide does not imply public right-of-way. One exception is land owned by International Paper Company, and section 30 details the special restrictions for those lands and descibes how to obtain permits to enter them.

Burn combustible trash and carry out everything else.

Most *wildflowers and ferns* mentioned in the text are protected by law. Do not pick them or try to transplant them.

Safety in the Woods

It is best *not to walk alone*. Make sure someone knows where you are heading and when you are expected back. Sign in wherever there is a registration booth at a trailhead.

Carry *water* or other liquids with you. Not only are the mountains dry, but the recent spread of *Giardia* makes many streams and ponds suspect. I have an aluminum fuel bottle especially for carrying water; it is virtually indestructible and has a deep screw that prevents leaking.

Carry a small *day pack* with insect repellent, flashlight, first aid kit, emergency food rations, waterproof matches, jackknife, whistle, raingear, and a wool sweater, even for summer hiking. Wear layers of wool and waterproof clothing in winter and carry an extra sweater and socks. If you plan to camp, consult a good outfitter or camping organization for the essentials. Better yet, make your first few trips with an experienced leader or with a group.

Always carry *a map and compass*. You may also want to carry an *altimeter* to judge your progress on bushwhack climbs.

Wear unbreakable *glasses* when bushwhacking. The risk to your eyes of a small protruding branch makes this a necessity.

Carry *binoculars* for birding as well as for viewing distant peaks.

Bears have become a problem throughout the Adirondacks in areas where campers have concentrated. Keep all food in sealed containers and hang all food overnight in "bear bags," suspended on a rope trough between two trees at least 15 feet apart, with the bear bag at least 10 feet from the ground. Do not keep food in your tent. Bears are not usually a problem during the daytime and only at night if they detect food. If bears do come near your campsite, clanging pots and pans may scare them away.

Use great care near the *edges of cliffs* and when *crossing streams* by hopping rocks in the streambed. Never bushwhack unless you have gained a measure of woods experience. If you are a novice in the out-of-doors, join a hiking group or hire the services of one of the many outfitters or guides in the north country. As you get to know the land, you can progress from the standard trails to the more difficult and more satisfyingly remote routes. Then you will really begin to discover the Adirondacks.

Overview

BEFORE FOLLOWING ANY of the routes in this guide, you might wish to drive the roads that circle the region and become acquainted with the hills and mountains you will explore and the historically significant sites you will visit. You could drive the encircling roads in two hours, but allow at least a day. If you stopped at all the attractions listed in the Overview, you could even stretch your introduction to the area into a two-day trip. The region is small but its destinations are numerous.

Arbitrarily, this overview starts in Speculator, at the junction of NY 30 and 8, but if you are coming from the Northway (I-87) on the east, pick up the circle by following NY 8 west through Chestertown, Wevertown, and Johnsburg. Peaceful Valley Road, on the northeast side of the circle, intersects NY 8 east of Sodom, joining the circle there.

Starting in Speculator, check the town's Office of Tourism information booth 0.5 mile south of the village on NY 8/30. It is open in summer and on occasional weekends throughout the year, and it provides up-to-the-minute travel and recreational information.

Follow NY 30 as it climbs north out of Speculator through forests owned and logged by International Paper Company. You will cross the Jessup River, which empties into Indian Lake.

A mile north of the Jessup, Mason Lake comes close to the west side of the road. Four miles north of the Jessup, you will see Lewey Lake on the west and Indian Lake on the east. Both have excellent state campsites and give access to many walks described in the guide (see sections 45 through 58).

Next, NY 30 heads east of north to follow the shore of Indian Lake. The trails described in this book are all to the east of this highway and the lake and so do not include Snowy and Squaw mountains, which loom to the west. Note the peculiar shape of their rock faces; they will be good landmarks to help orient you to the landscape you will see later when you climb to the tops of some of the mountains.

Indian Lake lies in a deep valley created by faults in the ancient precambrian rock base that constitutes the Adirondack Mountains. The valley points to the northeast, a direction typical of faults in the region. Indian Lake is not a natural lake; a dam controls the level of the water

Buckhorn Pond

backing up the Indian River to create the fourteen-mile-long flow. There can be drastic changes in the shoreline between spring and fall.

On most of your trip north along NY 30 you will find the highway is far enough from the lake that you will only glimpse it occasionally. Most of the shoreline is state land. The exceptions are a small section on the east shore within a mile of the dam and several stretches on the west shore where you will find clusters of cottages to rent among the private camps. Most of these are not visible from the road. If you are looking for accommodations, stop when you reach Indian Lake village at the head of the lake, further on. The town clerk's office in the middle of the village will be able to give you current information about lodging in the area.

Continuing north you will drive through the small community of Sabael. It is about 4 miles south of Indian Lake village. Sabael was named for a Penobscot Indian, Sabael Benedict, who settled in the area during the Revolutionary War. He had a hunting and fishing camp on Thirteenth Lake. Legends surround his death, which occurred when he left that camp in 1855 to head back to his home on Indian Lake. At the time he was reputed to be 104 years old. There were claims that another Indian or even Sabael's own son murdered him for the gold he was supposed to have accumulated from the sale of furs or from a hidden mine. Legend has it his protests are still supposed to account for the wailing shrieks which arise from the frozen lake on windy winter nights.

North of the narrows on Indian Lake, where the road has been widened into a scenic vista, stop and sort out some of the mountains to which this guide will lead you. The huge complex to the southeast is Bullhead Mountain, with John Pond ridge in front of its northern flanks. Ranging south of Bullhead are Puffer, Humphrey, Kunjamuk, and Moose mountains.

As you descend the hill toward Indian Lake village, notice Big Brook Road, a sharp right turn immediately at the foot of the hill. That road, which crosses man-made Lake Abanakee on a causeway, gives access to many destinations including Kings Flow, Chimney Mountain, and the Kunjamuk Road (sections 59 through 74).

Turn east at Indian Lake village to follow NY 28 toward North Creek. You are on the "new" over-the-mountain road. The route was steep and tortuous for early visitors, one of whom described the trip west from North River in 1859 as being along a road "so poor and full of large boulders that most of the passengers found it more comfortable to walk than to ride in the three-seated wagon or any of the three buckboards."

For nearly two decades previous to 1859, the road followed a circuitous route surveyed in 1841 from North Creek, southwest through Christian Hill, so named because the small community contained three churches. The road passed Thirteenth Lake and turned west beside Puffer Pond to Kings Flow, where it turned north and followed Big Brook. Later, the Ordway Road was laid out from Christian Hill and along the present Chamberlain Road to the general area of the present NY 28. This mountainous route was an important link in the stage road to the growing resort community at Blue Mountain Lake to the northwest.

The first automobile to travel the road west from North River was a 1905 Winton which made the trip in 1906, its drivers guided by the new USGS surveys as road maps.

So few inhabitants lived along the stretch of road, which was then in Essex County, but isolated from it, that the county saw no reason to keep it in repair. More than a decade of struggling was necessary before a land exchange was made and Hamilton County acquired the eastern part of the road. Finally, in 1916, the present route was paved, connecting Indian Lake with the railroad at North Creek.

NY 28 descends to the Hudson River and provides an unusually scenic drive southeast to North Creek. A mile south of the highway's approach to the Hudson, Thirteenth Lake Road heads southwest, giving access to adventures described in sections 77 through 90.

Continue on NY 28 and turn right, or south, on the road that is 0.8 mile south of Thirteenth Lake Road. The road leads to the Barton Mine, an open pit garnet mine located in a valley on the northwest side of Gore Mountain. The mine on Gore was closed in 1984 and a new operation started on Ruby Mountain.

Four generations of the Barton family have run the mine continuously for the last one hundred years. The old mine site is open to visitors from 9 a.m. to 5 p.m. six days a week and from 11 a.m. to 5 p.m. on Sunday, from the last week in June through Labor Day. A nominal fee is charged for the tour, which includes a lecture and slide show. At the mine entrance a mineral shop displays minerals and faceted garnets. Tours of the mine are scheduled from the shop. A visit will acquaint you with the mining process and the garnets that are found throughout the Garnet Hills (sections 77 through 84).

It is a handsome 5-mile side trip to the mine. There is a winter overlook 3.2 miles in from NY 28 toward the mountains northeast of the Hudson. From the mill area the view west toward Puffer and Peaked and Slide mountains is almost as impressive as the view from the top of Gore. On your return to North River, look back west to the handsome range of cliffs on Ruby Mountain, which seems to hang above the small village.

Continue east on NY 28, through North Creek, and turn south on Peaceful Valley Road toward Gore Mountain Ski Area. Along this road, there are views back to the north to the peaks northeast of the Hudson. In winter it can be jammed, for the area attracts both downhill and cross-country skiers. The new gondola operates weekends from July through August, and Fridays as well as weekends through and including Columbus Day. If it is a clear day, the ride to the top is well worth the $4.00 fee charged as of this writing. There are discounts for children and senior citizens. Walk 300 yards to the fire tower for the best vantage from which to study the mountains and valleys of the wilderness area.

The cliffs and exposed rock on Ruby, Peaked, and Slide mountains are visible in the northwest. South of the massive Bullhead Mountain and across the valley of the East Branch of the Sacandaga is Puffer Mountain. Study its huge cliffs, which range across the face of the mountain below the summit. Puffer is only 111 feet lower than Gore, and it, too, has magnificent views. If you attempt the difficult bushwhack to the cliffs on Puffer (section 74), you will appreciate the insight gained from this view on Gore's summit.

Gore has striking views of the High Peaks to the north and on a clear day, Snowy and Squaw mountains are visible to the west. South of west, County Line and South Pond mountains block more distant views. Farther south, across the East Branch, you see the range of mountains which rim NY 8: the Blue Hills, Black Mountain, and Eleventh Mountain (sections 11, 13, 21, and 22).

From Gore, continue south on Peaceful Valley Road to NY 8 at Sodom, a hamlet whose intriguing biblical name was imported with its first settlers, who came from another Sodom in Putnam County in southern New York State.

For 20 miles southwest to the intersection with NY 30 and the confluence of the East Branch of the Sacandaga with the Main Branch, the road passes by very few homes and farms. From NY 8 you can reach many of the walks described in *Discover the Southeastern Adirondacks* as well as those of sections 1 through 25 of this guide.

The first mountain to the west of Sodom is Eleventh, the third highest in the region; it rises 1600 feet above the road. If you make the drive in early spring, look north across the farm fields that border NY 8, 2.5 miles west of Bakers Mills. A small waterfall plunges over 300 feet from the shoulder of Eleventh Mountain. By summer it will be dry, but the rocks near the head of the falls are an enticing destination (see section 22).

As you continue west, the road climbs to a height-of-land, 1950 feet above sea level, with the spot indicated by a Forest Preserve marker. You may have begun to wonder why Eleventh Mountain and Thirteenth Lake were so named. The original township map holds the answer. Eleventh is "the" mountain in the Eleventh Township, Thirteenth Mountain and Thirteenth Lake are the notable features of the Thirteenth Township, and Gore Mountain is the mountain in the gore or small strip between the Twelfth and Fourteenth townships.

West of Eleventh Mountain, a small clearing marks the Siamese Ponds Trailhead. Only a state historical marker denotes the access, which leads to routes in sections 18 through 21 and 25. Every other access north of NY 8 is unmarked. Sections 1 through 17 describe the unmarked routes to the many mountains and valleys north of the East Branch of the Sacandaga.

The brilliant reds of maples and the golds of birch light up the East Branch valley in late September and early October. There are many places along the road to stop and enjoy the river and the mountains that rim it. Through the trees, you will catch glimpses of cliffs which edge the steep faces of the mountains. This valley too was created by erosion along an enormous fault in the ancient rock base.

Look for the state reforestation area 2.7 miles southwest of the Siamese Ponds Trailhead. Here new growth conceals Fox Lair (section 14), a perfect place to stop for a picnic beside the East Branch.

About 9 miles beyond Fox Lair look sharply to the north for the road to the abandoned community of Griffin and the only bridge across the East Branch. The road, 2.5 miles east of NY 30, gives access to sections 1 through 4.

Continuing on NY 8, you reach the bridge over the Main Branch, where you turn north on NY 8/30. In 1.5 miles a small white sign marks the Auger Falls picnic spot on International Paper Company lands. Sections 26 and 27 describe the beautiful gorge by Auger Falls and Auger Flats. Above Auger Flats, notice the rock slide on Macomber Mountain. It has a marvelous view and is one of this guide's easiest bushwhack climbs (see section 28).

Farther north, Old Route 30 used to make a loop with NY 8/30 on the east side of the Sacandaga. The southern end of the loop was reached by a connecting bridge which is just over 2 miles north of Auger Flats. The bridge is now closed and probably will not be replaced. You can make a side trip on Old Route 30 by turning right at the northern end of the former loop, 5 miles north of Auger Falls. See the chapter on the Main Branch of the Sacandaga for details of the drive along the now dead-end Old Route 30 and the excursions accessible from it.

Continuing once again on NY 8/30 north toward Speculator, you parallel the Sacandaga. To the north you see the broad valley of the Kunjamuk River, which flows into the Sacandaga south of Speculator. The Kunjamuk Valley stretches north for twelve miles; the first old road north from Speculator to Indian Lake followed that valley. Parts of the old Kunjamuk Road are trails described in this guide. Its northern terminus is on Big Brook Road, nearly 18 miles away. Both this remarkably flat route and the trails along the East Branch in the deep wilderness interior on the way to the Siamese Ponds are anomalies. They provide level hiker's highways and access to many points on the interior. Traveling along them gives a distinctly different experience from the majority of routes in this guide. In fact, walking along the two long routes beside the often sluggish streams can almost be dull, but is easy to appreciate why early road builders chose them for the main routes.

Follow these hiker's highways to the heart of the Siamese Ponds Wilderness Area, but use them as access to the guide's other walks. The treks to the birch-covered cliff-faced mountains, through boulder-strewn steep valleys, or along the brooks surging from the wilds between the mountains will better give you the true flavor of this deep wilderness.

Along the East Branch of the Sacandaga

"WET BEGINNINGS" IS the perfect description for one of the best groups of walks in this guide. Nearly every route examined in section 1 through 25, from Griffin past Eleventh Mountain on the north side of NY 8, requires crossing the East Branch of the Sacandaga by some means. Because of this, the following warnings apply.

In dry summer weather, and especially during a drought, it is usually an easy matter to hop stones and rocks in the river's bed and remain dry. Locations appropriate for such crossings are noted in the text.

Hunters often use cables to cross the East Branch and while several safe ones can be found near some trailheads, I do not attempt or recommend cable crossings. The cables are not installed by the DEC, but by hunters for their own use. However, the state does not actually disapprove of them, possibly because of the problems created by the lack of hikers' bridges.

Fishermen safely wade the East Branch, even in high spring water. For many years sites near County Line and Shanty brooks were forded by horse and wagon, driven first by loggers and later by outfitters who packed supplies into the wilds for hunters and fishermen. Hikers might want to use rubber boots to cross in these spots, but they would probably be better equipped with an old pair of sneakers, which can be exchanged for dry boots after crossing.

Few people have found suitable conditions and locations for crossing the East Branch in late winter. Winter crossings are dangerous, and therefore snowshoe and ski-touring trips involving them are not included in this guide. Of course, on those routes where no crossing is required, winter treks are suggested if appropriate.

Only with these warnings is it possible to describe the magnificent valleys and mountains north of the East Branch of the Sacandaga. If conditions are not perfect or you are worried about getting wet, there are trips to this range that do not involve wet beginnings: try sections 1 through 4, reached by an old road bridge; or sections 14 and 18, easy walks on the south side of the river, or sections 21 through 25, in areas between the upper reaches of the river and NY 8.

If you study the topographical map of the mountains before you set out, you will begin to feel the complicated grandeur of the range, with its rows of nearly parallel, glacially deepened fault valleys. This range, as well as the one on the south side of the East Branch and NY 8, was formed about 1.1 billion years ago at the edge of a dome whose uplift was caused by a large intrusion of anorthosite. Along the range the anorthosite is clearly identified by the large blue crystals of labradorite that characterize it. Eleventh Mountain, located at the head of the valley, is composed of sediments that have been intruded by some slightly younger granitic materials and then subjected to extreme metamorphism.

A long fault developed through the ridge. This zone of weakness became the valley of the East Branch. Centuries of erosion by water and glacial activity scraped the valley, leaving the steep rock faces that edge the river today. The details of the landscape are new, but the rock on which the features have been carved is ancient, even in geological terms.

Similar geological events created the row of parallel valley streams that flow from the north into the East Branch. These too may follow fault lines and have been deepened by erosion, cutting the long ridge beside the East Branch into the row of individual mountains you now see. North-south configurations of the valleys are almost constant throughout the area. Major intrusions, dikes, have the same north-south orientation. This tends to create the sharp clefts on the rock faces of the mountains north of the river.

If you drive along NY 8 in winter, you will be able to see clearly the rocks, cliffs, and escarpments that face the range. In this chapter you will find details of bushwhacks that lead to most of them.

A geological appreciation of the area will not only enhance your enjoyment of the walks and climbs, but also will aid in route planning and bushwhacking. It can provide the essential clues to search for the simplest and gentlest routes to the cliffs and exposed rock faces in the following sections.

1 Griffin

Waterfalls, picnic sites, short paths, fishing, swimming

The first road bridge to cross the East Branch of the Sacandaga was built about 1840 to serve the community that grew to become Griffin. A narrow iron successor is still the only bridge across the river, and it gives you access to several handsome short paths beside the largest waterfall on the East Branch. Nearby, you will find shady picnic spots and pools for swimming. The bridge also gives you access to an old road leading to Auger Falls on the Main Branch of the Sacandaga and to footpaths up two stream valleys that etch the mountains to the immediate north (see sections 2 through 4).

To reach the Griffin bridge from the intersection of NY 8 and 30 north of Wells, follow NY 8 northeast for 2.5 miles, where a dirt road leads north along the hemlock-covered bank guarding the East Branch to the bridge. After crossing the river, park and walk back to the bridge to admire the

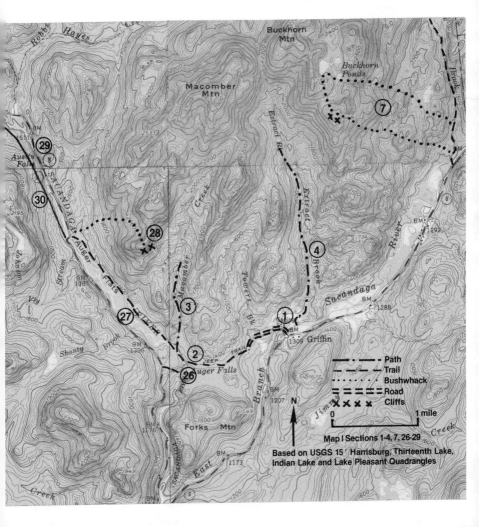

— · — · —	Path
— — —	Trail
· · · · · ·	Bushwhack
= = = =	Road
✗ ✗ ✗ ✗	Cliffs

0   1 mile

Map I Sections 1-4, 7, 26-29
Based on USGS 15′ Harrisburg, Thirteenth Lake,
Indian Lake and Lake Pleasant Quadrangles

gorge and the falls just downstream and to review some of Griffin's history.

Downstream, you will see the Griffin Falls glistening below towering hemlock. Look on the north side of the bridge for the beginning of a footpath that will lead you downriver for a better look. The path and its several branches extend no more than 400 yards west, but will take you to several picnic spots and a swimming hole below the falls.

Look upstream, past the rapids, to the quiet water. You are sure to spot a fisherman here. This site, with its narrow crossing and its surge of water, attracted the first settlers. They saw huge stands of hemlock like the one you see on the south side of the river, but they also saw hillsides covered with gigantic pines. Pine, the best building lumber, and water to float the logs to sawmills in Wells, brought the first men here in 1835. The first road for settlers, who called their little community Moon Mills, was laid out from Wells in 1838 and 1839.

The first of several dams was built across the East Branch at the head of the rapids. When the impounded water was released, the flow was large enough to flood logs through the rock-strewn river to Wells. Soon, the river was harnessed to create power for mills built on the site. Several different families ran sawmills near the head of the rapids and the community grew slowly until the 1870s.

By that time, the pine had all been cut from nearby forests, and hemlock had been stripped from most of the more accessible hillsides in southern New York and the southern Adirondacks. It finally became profitable to bring skins from all over the United States to this remote community on the side of the East Branch for tanning, for here they would be near a source of tannin. In the next decade, all the hemlock for miles around were felled and their bark peeled. Huge mills were built to grind the bark and leach tannin from it, and sheds were constructed to hold the large tanks in which the skins were pickled. In order to produce fine shoe leather, they had to cure in the acid solution for six months.

The firm of Catlin and Hunt from Wells was the first to build a tannery at Moon Mills. In 1872, they erected a mill complex which stretched along the north side of the Sacandaga from the bridge almost to Extract Brook, which is upstream of the Griffin rapids. Overnight, Moon Mills became a boom town with three hundred residents. Stores, hotels, homes, blacksmith shops, and offices were added to the tannery buildings that covered the hillside north of the bridge.

You can poke around in the woods north and east of the bridge and find the foundations of many of the buildings. In the first structure, hides were "sweated" to remove the hair. Next east are the ruins of the two-story generating building. Little is left of the drying sheds or the offices that lined the road along to the east, but the outlines of the huge tannery shed are clearly visible in the dense forest between the marshy area and a small hill on which workers' homes were built. The tannery shed was 409 feet long and outlines of some of the rectangular vats are still visible, as is the location of a flume that carried water from a dammed pond north of the tannery shed through the tannery, finally flushing wastes into the river. The tannery required huge amounts of water to leach the tannin from the hemlock bark and to flush wastes from the cured skins. A pipe carried water from Tower Brook to the tannery pond.

Between the site of the present bridge and the confluence of Extract Brook, the East Branch was dammed, impounding a mile-long flow from which water was released to float logs downstream in the spring to mills in Wells.

Griffin Gorge

About the time the tannery was built, Stephen Griffin II, a lumberman from Essex County, acquired timber rights to 43,000 acres near Johnsburg. In 1877, he built the Oregon Tannery at a site on the East Branch of the Sacandaga, 8 miles to the east of Griffin (see section 14). He also acquired timber rights to land near Moon Mills and soon moved the headquarters of his tanning empire from Oregon to this site, which was quickly renamed Griffin.

By 1882, Griffin had made his fortune. He leased his tannery to Rice and Emery and Company, a Massachusetts firm that enlarged the Griffin mill into one of the two biggest in New York State. Griffin next sold his timber rights to Morgan Lumber Company of Glens Falls, the company that later became International Paper Company. He then retired to Glens Falls, but the community that adopted his name continued to grow. The prosperity was short-lived. By the end of the decade, most of the hemlock had been harvested from the surrounding forests, and a new process of tanning leather using synthetic chemicals had been developed. The tannery operation at Griffin ceased in the early 1890s, and the property was sold with the understanding that all the buildings would be removed by 1901.

Now almost no signs of the original community remain, and only a few homes and cottages survive. Most notable is the Girard Hotel on the south side of NY 8, about 0.5 mile east of the road to Griffin. The foundations of the tannery are concealed by the forest that is returning the region to wilderness. Only the giant pines are lacking.

To learn more of this wilderness enterprise, read the chapter on the "Lost Community of Griffin" in the *History of Hamilton County*, by Ted Aber and Stella King.

2 Auger Falls Road

Old road, easy footpath, waterfalls, cross-country skiing, picnic sites, campsites
2 miles one way, 2 1/2 hours round trip, minimal vertical rise

There has been a road west from Griffin to Auger Falls on the Main Branch of the Sacandaga since the middle of the nineteenth century. That road led to a ford across the river immediately upstream from the falls. At some unknown point, it was extended north of the falls along the Main Branch to connect with Old Route 30.

You will surely want to follow the road west from Griffin to the path that leads along the ledges above the falls. You may even want to continue on it north of the falls alongside the Main Branch for 0.5 mile. You could venture all the way north on the road to a sand and gravel pit at the southern end of Old Route 30. From Macomber Creek crossing north, the land is owned by International Paper Company and a permit to cross is required (see introduction to Chapter III—The Kunjamuk). Summer walking here is none too pleasant, but the route is a snowmobile trail which also makes good cross-country skiing. For this, you might want to leave a car at either end, since the road is not plowed west of Griffin Bridge. The northern end of the road now ends in a pit that supplies International Paper Company with sand and gravel to improve its woods roads. See the chapter on the Main Branch of the Sacandaga for a description of the access from that end of the Auger Falls Road.

For trips in any other season, start at the Griffin Bridge. You will find the walk due west along the dirt road to Auger Falls and the Main Branch most delightful. Assuredly, there is no easier and no shorter trek to enjoy both deep woods and a magnificent waterfall.

Because some of the land west of Griffin is privately owned, the road is open to vehicular traffic for a distance of 0.5 mile beyond the bridge. However, I recommend crossing the bridge to park on its north side and then walking the entire distance. The road turns left at the bridge, quickly leaving the East Branch of the Sacandaga, which swings south. After 0.5 mile you will come to a dilapidated bridge over Towers Brook. Even if you choose to drive the first 0.5 mile of scrub forest to this bridge, you will have to leave your car here, where parking is poor.

Beyond the brook, the forest deepens into an almost pristine hemlock grove. After walking 1.5 miles west of Griffin, you should begin to hear the roar of Auger Falls. Soon the road approaches the Main Branch. Ahead the water runs swiftly, and a sign posted on the river's bank bears a warning to boaters who might venture from the quiet water of Auger Flats, upstream: "Hazardous Gorge Area: Sheer Cliffs, Swift Water, Slippery Footing."

Remember these cautions when you leave the roadway to follow the footpath south along the falls area. This path, which is informal and unmarked, leaves the road on the left as you first approach the river. For most of the way, you are safely back from the surge of water as it channels into the narrow gorge. Even in low water, the torrent keeps the moss-covered rock edges slippery, so do be careful if you stray from the path.

One hundred yards from the road you will see that the gorge turns sharply to the west, enabling you to see the first of its steep cliffs. The path continues through deep, dank woods beside the gorge, and a thick carpet of moss caps the rocks edging the river. The path is almost level along the ledges; the river falls steeply away below you. The roar of tumbling water contributes to the sense of isolation in the dark gorge.

I have enjoyed several high perches on the hemlock-covered cliffs above the falls. Each is accessible from the path and each gives a different perspective of the gorge and falls. Auger Falls is actually a series of short cascades that drop over 100 feet, tracing an S through the sharp curve of the gorge. Unfortunately, there is no safe place from which to see the whole series of falls at once. Nor can you see the entire sweep of rock cliffs at once because the walls are so sheer and the gorge so narrow.

Return north on the falls path to the road. If you have time you might want to continue north along the Main Branch of Sacandaga. The road stays close enough to the river so you can appreciate the 0.5-mile stretch of rapids upstream from the falls. Halfway along, there is a good snowmobile bridge over Macomber Creek. The bridge is one of hundreds in the Adirondacks that have been built of wood in the past decade to make it safe for snowmobiles to cross large streams. Envious hikers, who also appreciate the bridges, long for just one or two across the East Branch of the Sacandaga.

As the water of the Sacandaga quiets into the soft flow of Auger Flats, the road pulls away from the swamp, and there is a dramatic change in the forest. The road continues north another 2 miles to the sand pit at the south end of Old Route 30 through forests that have been disturbed by logging and fires. The roadway is so choked with brambles and so far from the river that summer hiking along this section is not really desirable.

There are several campsites and fire rings near the roadway on the stretch beside the rapids. The one closest to Macomber Creek is probably the least damaging to the fragile gorge. In spite of the fact that you are on the edge of wilderness here, when you are away from the falls you can hear traffic on NY 30, across the river.

The one-way trek from Griffin to Old Route 30 is 4 miles. A round-trip walk between Griffin and the falls is also about 4 miles. Extending the falls walk to include the stretch beside the rapids will give you a little over 5 miles of very pleasant walking. Either way, you will want to allow more than four hours for the round trip; you will need that much time to picnic and enjoy the falls.

3 Macomber Creek
Footpath

Macomber Mountain and Macomber Creek may have been named for Benjamin Macomber, a mail driver who made the weekly mail run from Northville to Lake Pleasant over the roughest of mountain roads from the late 1820s through the 1840s. Spafford's *Gazetteer* of 1824 described the area as a "wild waste of mountain and swamp lands, abounding with small lakes."

Today, Macomber Creek is just as wild and is a good place to sample the rugged forests of yesterday. To reach the informal path beside the creek, walk west from the Griffin bridge (section 1) on the Auger Falls Road, and then north beside the Main Branch of the Sacandaga for a total of 1.8 miles to the snowmobile bridge over Macomber Creek (section 2). Immediately south of the bridge a small informal path heads north, to the right, along the creek. You may occasionally lose it as you walk, but you will not lose your way, for hunters have cut the path close to the creek.

The creek bed and pathway are fairly level for the first 0.2 mile. It takes less than ten minutes to walk to the place where the creek tumbles out of the mountain valley, making refreshing rapids and falls. Quite near the first rapids, the informal path seems to disappear. It crosses to the west side to avoid the steep hemlock-covered bank on the east. Use the rocks as steppingstones to get across. Five minutes later, as the creek bends, the informal path disappears again. Recross the creek, hopping rocks, and find the path on the east side.

It is possible to follow the path for more than 1 mile north, although it continues to disappear periodically. Walking along it is a lovely way to enjoy the creek and the heavily wooded forests in its valley. Eventually the path fades altogether, probably hiding the hunter's lair to which it obviously must lead. The creek could continue to guide you farther up the valley toward the summit of Macomber. Both path and creek can lead you on a 700-foot climb more than 2 miles into the wilderness from the Main Branch of the Sacandaga. That trek, round trip, will require at least three hours. Be sure to allow another two and a half hours for the trips between Griffin and the path's beginning.

4 Extract Brook
Old road, easy footpath, snowshoeing

Extract Brook flows into the East Branch of the Sacandaga 0.5 mile east of the Griffin bridge (see section 1). An abandoned logging road parallels its west side. Originally, the road led for 2 miles past the site of the extract mill and the barking sheds of the Griffin Tannery to logging skids almost at the head of the valley. Today the road is a beautiful pathway.

To reach the path's start, walk right from the north side of the Griffin bridge on the dirt road. The area where the road turns left, north, beside the first house on the left, which was originally the Griffin schoolhouse, is private and posted. Do not continue on the road without obtaining permission from the landholder.

The continuing roadway is clearly marked with the corduroy that made the swampy areas passable in the wet weather. You reach state land 0.7 mile from the bridge. Sometimes the road wanders away from the brook, but most often it is quite close, making it most attractive for walking. The little brook runs gently here, and the clearest possible water tumbles over the huge white boulders. Steep mountains on either side shelter the small valley, making it the perfect place for the tall hemlocks that have reestablished themselves. Dark-loving mosses and liverworts carpet the creek's banks, maple and birch are interspersed among the hemlock groves, and giant boulders and glacial erratics dot the valley.

At 2 miles the course of the brook steepens and angles slightly west of north. But then, as the valley levels off, the road appears to stop near a site used by hunters and campers. Cross the brook and look about for the path that continues on the east. Here you will cross a small stream that enters Extract Brook from a draw south-southwest of Buckhorn Ponds. The path gradually becomes less distinct, but it is possible to follow it to within a mile of the saddle between Macomber and Buckhorn mountains.

There are many small cascades but no large falls on Extract Brook. While nothing about it is really distinctive, everything is particularly lovely; huge hemlocks, white boulders, clear water, and quiet are all ingredients for a secluded and easy wilderness stroll. Consider this footpath an excellent choice for a winter snowshoe climb or a spring nature walk. Going to the head of the valley and back is a lovely way to spend three or four hours.

Section 7 describes a challenging bushwhack route to the cliffs and ponds on Buckhorn Mountain and you should refer to that section for a description of the destination. An easier route to follow starts on the old road beside Extract Brook. From the bend in the road at 2.2 miles, it is a mile-long, 700-foot bushwhack on a course of 45 degrees magnetic, northeast to the cliffs. North of this line, you may encounter portions of a red-flagged route used by some fishermen to reach the ponds.

5   County Line Falls
Picnic site, old road, small waterfall, fishing

County Line Brook nearly parallels the boundary of Hamilton and Warren counties. About 2 miles north of where it empties into the East Branch of the Sacandaga, it falls through a small gorge into a deep pool that is a fisherman's delight. You can reach the gorge and falls by way of an old logging road that follows the brook's course. The pathway is also the access to sections 6, 7, and 8.

To find the path's start, stop about 0.33 mile west of the county line marker on NY 8 at one of three parking turnouts. Each is big enough for one or two cars. Below the westernmost turnout a path, or more accurately a slide, leads down to the East Branch, where two rusty cables indicate a crossing. In low water, the river's large stones make it easy to hop across to the north bank, where you can pick up the old road. There is a picnic site with tables on the small knoll between the path and the marshy confluence of the brook and river.

Avoiding the marshy area, the old road threads its way up the steep western side of the valley on the driest possible ground. Then for 0.2 mile the road stays fairly close to the brook. Beyond, it climbs up and clings to the steep, hemlock-covered bank, above and out of sight of the brook; you are rarely too far away to hear water tumbling over the huge boulders and echoing from the cliffs of Corner Mountain just up to the east.

For the last 0.5 mile to the falls area near the outlet from the Buckhorn Ponds, the diminishing roadway swings west toward higher ground to avoid an alder swamp. The 2-mile climb, which is gradual, should take you no more than an hour, and enough of the old corduroy survives to pave the few muddy stretches.

When you reach the outlet from the Buckhorn Ponds, leave the old logging road and bushwhack east a short distance through the alders. Keep to the southern end of the marsh to find the easiest route; it is quite brushy, but you reach County Line Brook in about 200 yards.

At the foot of the marsh, just as the brook begins to drop toward the gorge, you reach the small waterfall and deep pool. If the water is fairly low and the day is warm, stay in the gorge, hopping across boulders all the way back to the brook's closest approach to the path, scarcely 0.2 mile upstream from the East Branch crossing. You will find many small waterfalls, huge boulders that seem to block the way, cliffs shrouded with dark, overhanging hemlock, and glimpses of the huge pines that dot the cliffs on Corner Mountain above and to the east. There is also a marvelous string of pools that delights fishermen. Note that while the walk to the head of the gorge takes only about an hour, the rock-hopping trip downstream requires at least two.

6 County Line Brook/West Branch
Old road, campsites

The old logging road that follows County Line Brook into the mountains north of NY 8 (see section 5) does not end by the swamp near County Line Falls. After crossing the outlet from the Buckhorn Ponds it continues north another 1.3 miles, keeping to the high ground west of the swamps bordering County Line Brook. Then, when the brook splits into its two branches, the old logging road bears to the left, heading roughly north-northwest for another 2.2 miles along the brook's much smaller West Branch. The footpath ends 5.5 miles from NY 8 in a clearing. Although the clearing is nearly 500 feet higher than the highway, the grade is gentle and the climb to it should only take around three hours.

The clearing was a logging camp, and not too long ago you could still find piles of tanbark here near the brook. Because the path follows exactly the old logging road and because hunters have used the route in recent years to carry gear to the clearing by pack horse, it is easy to follow, level, and easy to walk. For the same reasons, it can be terribly muddy, even in dry times. There are several campsites along the path, and the clearing itself makes a good remote camping destination.

No road or path exists along the brook's East Branch, but if you set up camp this far in, you may wish to explore its valley. There used to be a flood dam for the spring log run less than 1 mile above its confluence with the West Branch. Log dams were left open after the spring run and only closed in late fall. Since this was a typical impoundment, never holding water in summer, it was named Dry Pond Flow. A shanty once stood on the west side of the East Branch, near the flow.

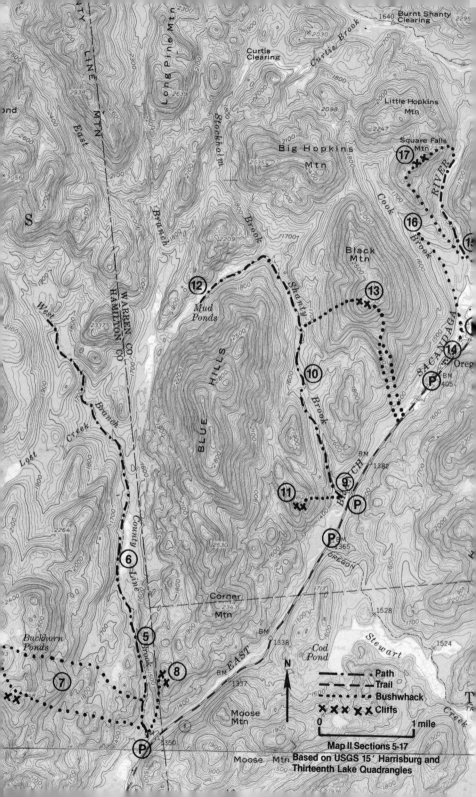

Map II Sections 5-17
Based on USGS 15' Harrisburg and
Thirteenth Lake Quadrangles

Path
Trail
Bushwhack
Cliffs

0   1 mile

7 Cliffs and Ponds on Buckhorn Mountain

Difficult bushwhack, impressive views

The trek to the cliffs and ponds on Buckhorn Mountain is the most difficult bushwhack on the north side of NY 8: the distance is great, the terrain is rugged, and navigation is complicated. The route described here requires a minimum of seven hours. For safety, your group of hikers should include at least three knowledgeable woodsmen.

The cliffs, one of your destinations, are visible from near the bridge over Lake Algonquin at Wells, from NY 30 about 1 mile north of the bridge, and from several points along NY 8. They appear to be quite close to NY 8. This deception made my early attempts at locating them most difficult. The cliffs are huge and actually range over a quarter mile across the smooth shoulder of Buckhorn. They are not vertical cliffs; rather the exposed rock is a slide over 200 feet in height. The shortest distance between them and NY 8 is over 1.5 miles as the crow flies, but they are so unexpectedly large and distant that it is easy to be tricked into believing they are closer and more accessible than they really are.

Begin the bushwhack at the County Line Brook crossing (section 5). Pick a compass course of 300 degrees magnetic. After a fifteen-minute walk, you should cross the outlet of an unnamed pond. The compass route leads up and down many small ridges; there are, disconcertingly, many more than the contour map shows. Keep to the north along the ridges to avoid descending too many draws. The woods are neither so brushy as to be difficult, nor so open as to be easy. The cliffs are visible from one or two breaks in the trees along the route. Do not be surprised if after one and a half hours of walking they appear as far away as they did at the start. The climb through the last 800 feet to the base of the cliffs is steep and strenuous. The cliffs rise 1300 feet above the East Branch, but even if you plan your route very carefully, you will end up climbing more than 1300 feet to reach them.

It takes at least two and a half hours after leaving the East Branch to climb to the top of the cliffs, but the impressive views make the effort worthwhile: Crane Mountain and Mount Blue on the east, Cathead to the south of Lake Algonquin, Hamilton Mountain and Mount Dunham to the southwest, and a great sweep of the East Branch valley to the southeast. Make sure you walk along the whole escarpment, as the views will change from east to west.

If you choose to return directly from the cliffs by compass, use a heading of a little less than 120 degrees magnetic. It is easier to intersect the County Line Brook path (section 5) than risk encountering the East Branch at an unknown point.

If time allows, continue to the north end of the cliffs, and then pick a compass route of 2 degrees magnetic down to the outlet of the Buckhorn Ponds. Follow the outlet to the ponds, being careful the stream you are paralleling swings northwest. If you are walking along its south side you will notice an intermittent stream entering from the southwest. Do not follow this false lead; make sure the stream you choose for a guide is flowing from the west or northwest.

Since the summer of 1978, there has been a large beaver dam at the outlet of the easternmost pond, creating one large pond where the USGS map shows two small ones. The walk northwest to the larger western pond is rough because the forest here is predominantly small spruce. Friends and I found the remains of a hunter's small log cabin on the south shore of the shallow western pond. After exploring the ponds area, retrace your steps along the outlet and then continue to follow it east. The map shows it dropping 700 feet in 0.6 mile. It is a fantastic plunge over slides and huge boulders. The forty-five minutes it takes to descend this stretch are the best part of the day's walk, and the roughest.

As the stream turns to the northeast, an open meadow and swampy area become visible. Leave the stream and pick a compass route east, 90 degrees magnetic. It takes you up and over another of the ridges that cover the mountain and then down to a lovely little pond. Beaver had at one time enlarged it, but now the surrounding meadows provide fairly dry walking. Circle the pond to the south, cross its outlet, and head 110 degrees magnetic. This route, south of east, takes you over one more ridge and then steeply down to the County Line Brook valley and the path. The rest of the hike is easy. It takes forty-five minutes to walk from the outlet to the pond, thirty minutes to walk from the pond to the path, and about fifteen minutes to walk south on the path to the East Branch crossing, where you began the bushwhack.

The approach to Buckhorn Ponds via the outlet, reversing the descent, has become so popular with fishermen that there is now a path east from County Line Brook as far as the unnamed pond. The path begins after a fifteen-minute walk north of the East Branch crossing.

Shanty Cliffs

8   Cliffs on Corner Mountain
Easy bushwhack

Step out onto a rock in County Line Brook and look north. The best spot is about 0.3 mile north on the County Line Brook path (section 5), where the path first approaches the brook. You should be able to see the large overhanging cliffs of Corner Mountain. Giant pines topping them give scale to their height and distance. The cliff tops are a little more than 300 feet above the brook and less than 0.5 mile away.

To bushwhack your way to the cliffs of Corner Mountain, cross the brook and head up the ridge to the north, climbing away from the lower cliffs. It is a mad scramble to the cliff tops, passing and climbing around many ledges on the way, but it should take no longer than forty minutes. The last 40-foot climb on the topmost ledge is slippery and very steep, but from the upper perch you have a marvelous view up the County Line Brook valley. The cliffs on Buckhorn Mountain dominate the western horizon and a part of the East Branch valley is visible to the southwest.

This is an easy bushwhack, in that the cliffs are not hard to find, but it is rather a scramble, and you should take care while climbing around the ledges. Wildflowers along the way make the ascent delightful. In summer one ledge is filled with the Puttyroot Orchid. When you return, be sure to head south along the ridge, so as to avoid the cliffs on the way down.

There are more cliffs higher up on Corner Mountain, some directly above the East Branch. An experienced bushwhacker might wish to continue around to the east at the 1800-foot contour to the first of them, and then cut northeast to those nearer the summit. The hulk of Georgia Brook Mountain looms directly south of Corner Mountain, and Harrington Mountain blocks distant views to the southeast. Nevertheless, there are at least a half-dozen perspectives from which to see the East Branch valley.

9   Shanty Brook Crossing
Trailhead, campsite, picnic site

As your first introduction to the Shanty Brook area, you should park along NY 8 at the new Shanty Brook trailhead turnout, walk to old road turnouts across the road on either side of it, stop for a picnic, and scout the East Branch crossing. If you arrive too late in the day to cross the river, you'll find several good campsites on the south bank, all quite close to the trailhead. If the river is too high to ford, you will find a secluded promontory from which to view its rushing waters.

Shanty Brook flows from the north into the East Branch of the Sacandaga, originating in the mountains that border the Siamese Ponds Wilderness Area. Its name has been given to a huge parking turnout (there is room for thirty cars) on the south side of NY 8, 8.7 miles northeast of the intersection of NY 8 and 30. The lot was designed to serve the multitude of snowmobile trails and routes to the south described in *Discover the Southeastern Adirondacks* as well as the routes north along Shanty Brook. The new turnout is close to the traditional Oregon Trailhead, the beginning of a major route south. However, few know of the paths to the north that have their beginnings near here.

On the north side of NY 8, 300 yards southwest of the parking area, a dirt road leads across an open field to a good dry campsite on the south side of the East Branch. Several paths lead from the campsite to the river.

The Shanty Brook path (sections 10, 11, 12, and 13) also begins on the north side of NY 8. Walk 250 yards northeast of the parking area to the dirt road that heads toward the river, circling a hemlock-shaped promontory that also makes a lovely camping spot.

One hundred feet along this road a small path drops down the steep bank to the river. This is the access to the Shanty Brook path. There are no signs and no indications of what is across the river. All you will see is two rusted old cables stretched from bank to bank. In low water the river can be forded here easily. On the north side is another campsite, the choicest in the vicinity, and the beginning of Shanty Brook path.

10   Shanty Brook Path to Stockholm Brook
Old road, waterfall, fishing, campsite

The path described in this section has traditionally been called the Shanty Brook Path. The route is an old logging road, well used in recent times by hikers, fishermen, and hunters. Only a few places at its north end could be difficult to follow, but, as the route has no markings for hikers, by the definition used in this guidebook, it is not a trail.

The Shanty Brook path commences at the crossing on the East Branch of the Sacandaga described in section 9. The crossing brings you nearly 220 yards downstream and west of the confluence of Shanty Brook. Shanty Brook's course probably follows a fault between the Blue Hills and Black

Mountain and parallels a line a little west of magnetic north.

The path follows the brook's west side for 1.2 miles, but there are few stretches along which the brook is visible. One of these occurs near the start, where the path comes close to the brook. It then swings west above the brook as the gorge surrounding it forms and begins to deepen. There is a beautiful waterfall at the head of the gorge, but to view it you will have to watch the path carefully. After walking 0.8 mile, you reach two wet places where the path curves. They signal the closest approach to the falls, which is roughly 100 yards to your right through the woods.

At the falls, water shoots over a twelve-foot-high wall of anorthosite, which forms the head of the deepest part of the gorge, a 200-yard-long ravine with nearly vertical walls. The pool below the falls is deep enough for swimming, though fishermen might protest. A lovely campsite can be found on the west bank above the falls, beneath an open hemlock grove.

For 200 yards above the falls, the brook is especially beautiful with slabs of rock worn in lines parallel to the stream's flow, creating sharp, angular ridges that define long and narrow pools. The pools are punctuated by small cascades. The smooth rock between the pools has a chain of mysterious patterns that can only be attributed to some mythological Big-Foot.

Mysterious Big Foot in Shanty Brook

Faults in the rocks lie in a north-south direction, the same direction as the ledge that forms the falls. The basic dike that was eroded to form the gorge is part of an intrusion into the Marcy anorthosite that is visible on the cliffs west of the gorge.

North of the falls and rapids there is a brief small, quiet flow, but in general, the brook courses over a gentle, boulder-strewn slope. For the next 0.5 mile the Shanty Brook path circles west, away from the wet, alder-filled shoreline. When the path swings east to the other side of the brook, a simple, rock-hopping cross, head 30 feet downstream to pick it up again. Neither part of the path is visible from the brook at this point, so you could easily become confused. Wet shores encourage rapid growth of alders and Joe-Pye weed, which conceals the path.

The path continues north on the east bank of Shanty Brook, where several blowdowns now obscure the footway. In 0.5 mile, the path emerges from a dense spruce thicket into the south end of a lovely vly, whose east shore it follows indistinctly before reappearing clearly beside the brook on the dry land north of the vly. The summit of Black Mountain (section 13) to the northeast is visible from the vly. It has been so long since beaver resided here that only a narrow stream of water winds through a grassy field. Above the vly the path continues clear and passable on the east side of the brook for another 0.5 mile and then crosses back to the west side. Your way at the second crossing is as difficult to locate as the first. The next 0.3 mile, to Stockholm Brook, is also very difficult to follow.

Allow twenty minutes to walk to the falls after crossing the East Branch, thirty minutes more for the walk to the first Shanty Brook crossing, another thirty minutes for the stretch to the vly, and forty minutes more to reach Stockholm Brook. Even if you stop for more than a half hour to enjoy the falls area, you can reach Stockholm Brook in two and a half hours. You can then either retrace your steps to the East Branch or continue toward Mud Ponds (section 12).

11   Shanty Cliffs on the Blue Hills

Moderate bushwhack, impressive views

If you look north and west from the Shanty Brook crossing (section 9), the first mass of mountains you see is the Blue Hills, which is actually a single mountain with a series of summit knobs. Between you and this mountain is a smaller knob whose fire-scarred open peak with an incredible chimney presents one of the most complex rock faces on any mountain on the north side of NY 8. These marvelous cliffs are easy to locate using a simple compass route and make a fine destination for a moderate bushwhack. Other high hills may have more distant views, but the panorama here is remarkable considering that the climb is less than 600 feet.

Starting at the Shanty Brook crossing, walk the Shanty Brook path (section 10) for less than five minutes through the brushy area near the East Branch of the Sacandaga as far as the path's first approach to Shanty Brook. When you reach a huge boulder on the west side of the path, begin the bushwhack. Set your compass for 260 degrees magnetic and start climbing. The course takes you over a small rise, across an intermittent stream, and then directly up to the cliffs.

Fires so completely destroyed the hillside's cover that the forest is entirely new growth, but the popple, grey and white birch, and striped maple are all large enough to make easy walking. The height of the mixed hardwood cover clearly indicates it has been close to three-quarters of a century since the fires. The forest floor has several varieties of *lycopodium*, including the *complanatum*, which is typical only in the northern Adirondacks and farther north.

A forty-minute climb over 0.7 mile from the Shanty Brook path yields the first of the open areas and views. You can walk beside the deep rock cleft and chimney that form the western face of the rock area. The cleft is 50 to 100 feet wide with vertical walls nearly 150 feet high.

A dike, an intrusion into the joint planes of the older anorthosite along a fault zone, created this special land feature. Since this dike was more readily eroded than the surrounding rock, it has worn away, leaving the nearly vertical chimney on the side of the hill. The dike is the largest in the Thirteenth Lake Quadrangle and occurs along a north-northwest to south-southwest strike, typical of this part of the southern Adirondacks.

The rock here is anorthosite, which is found throughout the Adirondacks although it is more typical of the High Peaks. The many small ridges on the rock slabs are dikes of harder rock. Look for the blue crystals of labradorite, which characterize anorthosite, embedded in the rock; some specimens here are remarkably large.

From the summit of this knob you can see Hamilton Mountain in the distant east across Corner Mountain. The huge complex to the south is Georgia Brook Mountain. While you are on top, examine the charred stumps of the huge pines that originally covered the hill and notice that almost no pine survive here today. Imagine the inferno required to burn the duff and top soil and completely clear the mountaintop!

On the return, reverse your compass heading to 80 degrees magnetic. If you maintain a direction a little under that heading, you will be certain to intersect the Shanty Brook path and not the swampy areas near the East Branch.

Since this bushwhack can be stretched to no more than half a day, you may want to combine it with a walk to the falls on Shanty Brook. Alternatively, if you are an intrepid bushwhacker, you can head northwest across the saddle between these cliffs and the Blue Hills. Here there are only a few exposed rock faces, and they are as difficult to find as needles in a haystack. One on the southwest face of Blue Hills is a lovely rock slide nearly 200 feet long. More adventurous hikers might even wish to climb from the south through the dike. This would be more challenging than the approach outlined, but it would also involve a long walk through a dense evergreen forest near East Branch.

12 Mud Ponds

Old road, campsites, fishing

Mud Ponds lie behind, or north of, the Blue Hills. Their outlet stream flows from the west and joins with Stockholm Brook to form Shanty Brook. A rough path used to follow the outlet for 1 mile from the Shanty Brook path to the ponds. The path is so unused that the way is best described as a bushwhack following the outlet. It appears that few fishermen have used this traditional route lately. Hikers will find few more remote, yet fairly accessible, campsites. To reach the ponds, follow the Shanty Brook path (section 10) to the confluence with Stockholm Brook and head southwest along Mud Pond Outlet. Bushwhack within sight of the outlet to the ponds.

Steep hills rise sharply from the first Mud Pond, whose brushy shores offer few camping spots. The best spot, at the head of this fairly shallow pond, is one of the area's few eyesores. Hikers should remember to carry out what is carried in. Rock climbers may wish to examine the formation on the pond's north side. The upper Mud Pond is also fairly shallow, with swampy shores and only one or two good campsites.

Even allowing time to search for the path, the walk from the Shanty Brook path to the ponds should take less than an hour, and the total trip from NY 8 only a bit more than three hours. The drop in elevation from the head of the upper Mud Pond to the confluence with Stockholm Brook is less than 20 feet, so this part of the walk is easy going.

13   Black Mountain Summit
Two moderate-to-difficult bushwhacks, views

Black Mountain rises 2732 feet above sea level, making it the smallest of the chain of major hills north of NY 8. However, the summits of its higher neighbors are all wooded. The open rock that crowns Black Mountain is higher than the exposed rock ledges on either Buckhorn or the Blue Hills, which lie to its southwest, or on Eleventh Mountain, which lies to its northwest. And none of these higher mountains have any better views.

Like that of its neighbors, Black's summit can be reached only by bushwhacking. Two routes are given here and the best adventure would be a circular walk combining both. Neither route can be considered easy.

One bushwhack approaches Black Mountain from the west. Walk north along the Shanty Brook path (section 10) past the falls to the vly. The walk should take about an hour and twenty minutes. The top of Black is clearly visible from the vly and should help you orient a compass course of 90 degrees magnetic, which will lead you directly to the summit. Allow nearly two hours for the steep climb of 1100 feet over less than 1 mile. The 500-foot-high summit knob, which rises steeply from the mass of Black, is surrounded by small ledges. On this approach you will have to wind around several. A return via the vly—which should take only an hour—is equally easy to orient, because the vly is quite visible from the summit at a heading of 270 degrees magnetic.

The second route to the summit is shorter and more direct. It involves bushwhacking from a point on NY 8 that is 1.4 miles east of the Shanty Brook parking turnout. Here there is plenty of room to park off the road on the north side near a sandy esker covered with scrub growth. This is also a good place from which to view the summit ledges.

Walk north across the ridge of the esker and descend to the East Branch and a crossing that is easily forded in low water. Then choose one of two parallel routes, 200 yards apart, which are suggested by natural features. The first is slightly south of the crossing and follows a small draw. Its course is 340 degrees magnetic toward the summit ridge. The other, a little north of the crossing, takes the same compass route up a gentler, more open ridge. Walking along the ridge, guided by a compass, is definitely easier, but parts of the draw are quite lovely and dramatic in a small way.

Either way, the first 0.2 mile on the compass course leads you over a small ridge and down into a valley that is so small it does not appear on the

Charcoal-preserved stump on Black Mountain

USGS map. Above the valley, both routes are consistently steep, offering a mile-long, 1300-foot climb to the summit.

Most of the forest cover at the foot of the mountain is open hardwood with occasional patches of thick, small evergreens. Hemlock edge the draw, and there brushy patches are more prevalent than on the ridge route. Five hundred feet from the top, the summit knob is ringed with a layer of dense spruce. The layer is not as dense or as wide on the western approach, but any bushwhack from the south and east will bring you into large thickets. They only *seem* impenetrable.

Above the spruce layer, the mountain is covered with small white birch and popple with lush fern pockets in the crunchy lichen cover. The parallel routes on the southern face lead to open areas that range below the summit. When you reach the first of these, head west to the summit, taking advantage of the openings. Bare rock patches become larger, the walking becomes easier, and the views begin to unfold before you reach the top.

All the natural signs tell of the turn-of-the-century fires that swept the mountain, baring the summit, which offers longer views of the lower East Branch valley than any other mountain along NY 8. Most of the peaks described in *Guide to the Southeastern Adirondacks* are visible beyond Harrington and Kettle mountains on the southeast.

The bushwhack up the south face requires over two hours and coming down somewhat less, so the round trip can be made in four hours. The trip in and out via Shanty Brook takes five and a half hours. The loop using both routes takes at least four and a half hours. None of the stated times makes an allowance for enjoying the views properly, however.

14 Fox Lair

Short paths, swimming, fishing, picnic sites, cross-country skiing, snowshoeing, camping

When the state of New York acquired the Hudnut estate, Fox Lair, it made accessible one of the most beautiful locations on the East Branch of the Sacandaga. The ruins of the estate, which was lavishly landscaped, spread across a small hill beside the river. The flagpole promontory beside the foundation of the main house commands a view north-northeast along the East Branch valley. Black, Big Hopkins, Little Hopkins, Square Falls, and Eleventh mountains are framed by a row of planted evergreens that border the sweeping drive.

If decaying ruins disturb your view of the wilderness, take heart; the wilderness has almost overcome. Tangled roots and rank new growth are interwoven across the sweeping staircases and garden walls. Young hemlock and spruce fill the untended gardens. Before long, all will be as overgrown as the other treasure beside the riverbank.

Fox Lair was also the site of the Oregon Tannery, one of the Adirondack's larger tanneries. It now lies partially concealed by junglelike thickets of branches. As overgrown as the foundations are, it is remarkably easy to discern the outline of the long tannery shed, the sluice for water, and the leaching house where all that remains of the huge leaching vats are their long iron straps.

There are a variety of ways to enjoy the site, which is accessible from either end of a road that passes through the estate grounds roughly parallel to NY 8. You can park at the southwestern end, off NY 8, 1.7 miles east of the Shanty Brook parking area, or at the northern end 0.8 mile farther along NY 8. This intersection is 2.6 miles west of the Siamese Ponds trailhead and leads into fields the state has reforested. The estate road makes a lovely short walk. Boulders bar vehicular traffic and the bridges are in need of repair.

Near the southern end of the estate, the East Branch flows through a small gorge with a deep swimming hole. There are trout in the river and many places to picnic along it. In winter the estate grounds are ideal for cross-country skiing and snowshoeing. A tour around the site, whatever the season, is an exploration into the Adirondack past.

The tannery site is between the river and the estate road at the southwestern end of the property. Walk 100 yards in on the road and around a small hill toward the East Branch. The westernmost foundations belonged to the old springhouse. The foundations for two long sheds range northeast along the river, and other walls indicate at least three more buildings.

Stephen Griffin, a lumberman from Essex County, acquired 43,000 acres in the towns of Johnsburg and Wells in the 1870s. His Oregon Tannery was built at the Fox Lair site in 1877. In 1880 he added the tannery at Griffin to his empire. Through the 1880s, Griffin lumbered the valleys along Shanty Brook, County Line Brook, and the East Branch of the Sacandaga. Tanbark from as far away as the present NY 28 was harvested and transported by horse and sled to the Oregon Tannery. The last working tannery in the area, it burned in March 1892.

Remember that others will wish to discover the few remains of the tannery that the wilderness now conceals. Please leave everything you find for others to discover.

Northeast of the tannery site stairs lead from the old road to a picnic spot overlooking a smooth, rock-lined gorge. Nearby can be found the ruins of an old bridge that served the farm communities north along Cook Brook. The principal buildings and gardens of the Hudnut estate were on the hill above, midway between the estate road and NY 8. As you walk north on the road through the estate you will see on your right several staircases and the main drive leading to the house site.

It is considerably more difficult to reconstruct the elegant past of the Hudnut estate from its remains than it is to visualize the tannery. The crumbled cement foundations of the 270-foot long main house give little clue to its rich past.

While Alexander Hudnut, a chemist from New Jersey, founded the family company, it was his son, Richard, who enlarged the business to include perfumes and a fashionable line of cosmetics and salons in London, Paris, and New York. His incredible fortune enabled him to acquire several homes and furnish them to suit his artistic tastes. He began buying land around Fox Lair before the turn of the century; it took ten years to acquire the entire estate.

The main house was three stories high with a huge double staircase and veranda across the front. Art, beauty, and the good life inspired Richard Hudnut, not the wilderness around him. He filled the house with furniture from the Continent, not with the plain, rustic Adirondack tables and chairs admired by other millionaires who fled to these woods to lead the simple life. Forty servants staffed the house. A Japanese teahouse and a nature house were built near the river, a golf course was laid out along the valley, and many barns were constructed to house carriages and animals. Willett Randall was hired to catch and care for a pair of foxes, which were kept as symbols of the estate. The foxes' lair was visible from the house, a huge aviary graced the porch, and other rare and exotic animals were housed in the barns. Every summer afternoon at five, dancing pigeons put on a show for famous guests who came from around the world.

With Richard Hudnut's death, the estate was given to the New York City Police Athletic League for a camp, and then finally to the state itself. The buildings were all burned so the land could become a part of the Forest Preserve.

The hillside where the main house stood is as beautiful as ever. Enjoy a picnic there and be entertained, not by dancing pigeons, but by hawks soaring in the north over Black Mountain.

15   East Branch Gorge and Square Falls
Short old road, easy footpath, waterfalls, fishing

The gorge on the East Branch of the Sacandaga is neither as wild nor as inaccessible as the more famous gorge on the West Branch, but these facts do not diminish its beauties. A walk along the path through the gorge is a highly desirable short excursion.

Park off NY 8 near the field that is about 2 miles southwest of the Siamese Ponds trailhead and 2.7 miles east of the Shanty Brook parking turnout. North of the field, an abandoned roadway heads northwest toward the East Branch. After a short walk to a small stream crossing, walk 50 feet west to pick up the path that continues north. It follows the East Branch upstream on a bank high above the river. A total of ten minutes walking will bring you to the first rapid and a cable crossing.

There are two ways to proceed; both are lovely. In low water, continue along the river's eastern shore, climbing high along its cliff-flanked border or hopping rocks in the riverbed where possible. On a pleasant, warm day, this is the best way to enjoy the river and the gorge. The rudimentary path on the east shore disappears after a few hundred yards, and soon pine- and hemlock-covered ledges on the shoulder of Eleventh Mountain drop so close to the river that walking this side becomes impossible. Then you will have to cross to the west shore path.

Alternatively, you can cross at the rapids and walk along the path on the west shore. It is possible to cross the river, dryly, at the base of the rapids; but again, low water is necessary. When the river is running high, hunters use the double cable. The footpath following the steep, hemlock-covered western bank is very special. From it there are views of all the rapids and cascades and the gorge walls, which rise between fifty and one hundred feet. A few truly magnificent pines edge the bank.

From the cable crossing 1 mile north to Square Falls (a waterfall near the head of the gorge) the footpath provides the best short walk described in this guide. It is a great place to photograph and because the ravine is so deep, midday light is favored to accentuate the many small falls. There are several deep pools and narrow rock troughs through which the river courses, lazily in summer, with fantastic spray in the spring. Some of the brook trout have to be hiding in those pools.

The falls are formed by a ledge of square-jointed rock, and their peculiar form must have inspired the name of the small mountain to the west, Square Falls Mountain. There are more smaller falls above the Square Falls, and the path continues along the shore beside them. Just below the steepest part of Square Falls Mountain, the river flattens out to a broad flow bordered with fields of Joe-Pye weed. Here the west shore path disappears.

The perfect trip through the gorge combines a walk along the west path with some rock-hopping in the river itself. A word of caution: poison ivy grows in several places along the river banks. Allow three hours for this very picturesque walk.

16 Cook Brook

Easy bushwhack, campsites

You will enjoy a bushwhack along Cook Brook if you are looking for a remote stream with camping sites that does not require a long walk. Cook Brook flows from the north-northwest in the valley between Black Mountain and Square Falls Mountain to join the East Branch of the Sacandaga near Fox Lair. Even a complicated bushwhacking loop that takes you 2 miles into the valley and then returns over Square Falls Mountain, for a total distance of 3.5 miles, takes no more than three and a half hours to walk.

You can fish and enjoy the brook and even do a bit of historical exploration in the farmsites that were located in clearings along the brook. The valley of Cook Brook was sparsely settled by farmers and lumbermen in the nineteenth century, but only the observant hiker will notice the remains of their homesites.

Leave your car off NY 8 at the northern end of the road through Fox Lair (section 14), 2.6 miles west of the Siamese Ponds trailhead and 2.4 miles east of the Shanty Brook parking turnout. Walk down the old road through the reforestation area to the large pines near the flood plain of the East Branch. Then head west toward the river and walk downstream about 50 yards to a beaver dam. This provides a semblance of a bridge for crossing.

On the other side, bear northeast on high ground over the shoulder of Black Mountain to intersect Cook Brook. Here you should be able to spot several overgrown old logging roads that appear to head away from the brook. There is also a hunters' path running along the west side of Cook Brook, which you should follow; it seems to be well used but disappears wherever there is a heavy new growth of underbrush.

Within 0.5 mile, the path intersects the first of two clearings. Each has distinct evidence of former habitation: stone walls and foundation pillars. One-quarter mile upstream from the second clearing you will come to a hunters' camp, and 0.2 mile past the camp, to a large beaver dam at the foot of Square Falls Mountain. There may be trout behind the beaver dam, but the stream is without exceptional falls or pools. However, there are many good camping places along Cook Brook; the best are near the abandoned farmsites.

In order to keep this an easy bushwhack, you should retrace your steps along Cook Brook, around Black Mountain, to your crossing opposite Fox Lair. A moderate bushwhack loop and a pretty extension of the walk involves skirting south of the beaver dam and climbing the shoulder of Square Falls Mountain. Choose a compass setting of 140 degrees magnetic to cross the shoulder and intersect the East Branch by the gorge. Then follow the rudimentary path downstream (section 15) to the crossing by the cables and continue to NY 8. Walk southwest 0.7 mile to your car.

17 Square Falls Mountain
Difficult bushwhack

The southeast face of Square Falls Mountain has a range of cliffs with good views, but unfortunately reaching them is difficult. There is no path so you must bushwhack most of the distance.

Start as for the gorge on the East Branch of the Sacandaga (section 15). Cross the river to the west side at the rapids below the cable. You will notice the path that follows the west shore of the river. A second path heads northwest from the cable, angling away from the river. Use it, if you can find it, and follow it for 0.2 mile. It is a poor route at best, so if you can not find it, begin your bushwhacking at the cable, heading northwest through the conifers bordering the river to a stand of white birch.

The birches mark the first of a series of well-developed ridges whose tops are easy to follow to the northwest. Near the 2000-foot contour, a large rock outcrop offers good views of Black Mountain and Cook Brook. There are several other rock outcrops along the ridge, which has a mixed hardwood cover, so all have good views in fall and winter.

The series of ridges curves toward the northeast and at the 2200-foot contour you reach a false summit. Continue north-northeast from the false summit, down into a small col, through some conifers and then a mixed forest to the true summit, covered with blowdowns. The overlook provides views of Eleventh Mountain, the East Branch valley, and south toward NY 8. The cliff that drops off here is precipitous but still covered with many trees, so appears much smaller from NY 8 than it actually is.

You have to climb 800 feet from the road and the crossing to reach the summit. But directly below the summit, the river is 150 feet above the level of the road. It really plunges through the gorge! From the summit, the most direct route to the river is straight down the eastern face of Square Falls Mountain, a sheer drop of 650 feet. It is possible to walk it easily, but be careful, for the way is steep, so steep, in fact, that the descent can be completed in as little as a quarter of an hour.

When you reach the river, turn south to walk downstream along the west bank. Soon you will pick up the path along the gorge, enabling you to complete the circuit back to the start. The loop is under 4 miles long and requires three and a half hours to walk. It is difficult both from the point of directing the bushwhack and because of the problems of circumnavigating the cliffs, but an avid bushwhacker will find it most rewarding.

18 East Branch Sacandaga Trail to Siamese Ponds Trail

Old road, trail, hiking, campsites, fishing, cross-country skiing
4.2 miles, 1³/₄ hours one way, 400-foot climb

The state-maintained trail north from Eleventh Mountain and NY 8 along the East Branch of the Sacandaga is the major north-south route to the interior of the Siamese Ponds Wilderness Area. Compared with all other trails in the area, this one along an abandoned road appears as a hiker's highway. A rock base, corduroy, and easy grades characterize much of the roadbed and provide an excellent modern trail.

The trailhead on NY 8 is almost 4 miles southwest of Bakers Mills and just under 13.5 miles northeast of the intersection of NY 8 and 30. The parking area is marked with a traditional state historical marker. The more modern trailhead sign stands hidden at the north end of the parking area. Department of Environmental Conservation (DEC) blue hiking and yellow ski-touring markers identify the trail.

A fifteen-minute walk will cover the distance northwest across the shoulder of Eleventh Mountain to the saddle 200 feet above the trailhead. Here, late afternoon sun provides the best illumination for the cliffs on the east of the trail and the stands of paper birch that shine most beautifully against the grey-green rock.

Now the roadway, or trail, descends 400 feet to the East Branch valley, 1.5 miles from NY 8. That gentle 400-foot descent is notorious among tired backpackers on the return from Siamese Ponds.

As you near the new bridge over Diamond Brook, stop for a moment to enjoy the views of cliffs on Diamond Mountain and the west face of Eleventh Mountain. Beyond, the trail winds through meadows and drying beaver marshes—in midsummer the tall grasses conceal the foot tread. You may have to search for the trail as you continue north. The trail does become clearer as it reenters the woods.

One mile north of Diamond Brook, you will come to a spot where there was a ford in the river and a road west toward Curtis Clearing (section 20). Beyond that, the trail passes through the scrubby new forests that are filling in Burnt Shanty Clearing. Along the trail in the 2-mile stretch between Eleventh Mountain and the fork to Siamese Ponds, the East Branch is occasionally visible, with rapids and small riffles breaking up the lovely reflections of otherwise still water. The East Branch has been stocked with good-sized brook trout, and there are many deep holes, which fishermen in your party will appreciate.

As you walk along, you might contemplate the history concealed in this wilderness. East of Diamond Brook, in the 1880s, John Sawyer lumbered and farmed and cut stove wood to serve the hotels to the east. Young spruce and apple trees in Burnt Shanty Clearing hide lands that were farmed after the land had been cleared and the lumbermen had left.

The names of the mountains and clearings only hint at the past. Several families settled in Curtis Clearing, west of the river, after 1865. Norman Curtis came first, followed by his brother, William, in 1870. Norman settled the eastern half of the land they purchased on the west side of the East Branch and built a house and a sawmill. William cleared a "goodly" farm 0.2 mile to the west and harvested between thirty and fifty tons of hay yearly in the clearing that bears the family name. Their two sisters, Eliza and Electra, each married a Hopkins; that family name survives as the Big Hopkins and Little Hopkins mountains. In the 1870s, their settlement to the west of the river was large enough to have a schoolhouse. William, who died in 1883, was buried in the family cemetery near his home.

Past Burnt Shanty Clearing, the trail edges close enough to the river that you might enjoy short side trips to it. The sensible road builders of yesterday did use the river valleys, but most often stayed far enough away to ensure a dry track. In summer, it seems as though every quarter mile of river has a resident kingfisher, guarding his territory with his rattling call.

A little more than 0.5 mile past the clearing, about 3.7 miles and a little over one and a half hour's walk from NY 8, there is a marked fork in the trail. The right fork, which was the old road, takes you 7.5 miles to the new trailhead past Old Farm Clearing at Thirteenth Lake (section 89). The left fork is fairly close to the river, but in summer you will still have to leave the trail to see the river's pretty slides. There are several open places not far from the river, if you choose to camp here rather than at the lean-to.

Notice how tall and straight the mature cherry trees grow beside the trail. Just 100 feet before the hikers' bridge, a path to the river leads to a shallow ford used by horseback riders.

Walking time for the 4.2-mile trek between NY 8 and the start of the Siamese Ponds Trail is less than two hours in either direction unless you are carrying a heavy pack. Then the return can take longer.

Cross-country skiers enjoy this wide track along the East Branch, but they find the shoulder of Eleventh Mountain a bit of a challenge and prefer to ski the route from north to south, starting at Thirteenth Lake. See section 89 for more details.

19 Siamese Ponds Trail

Trail, campsites, fishing, swimming, cross-country skiing
2.5 miles from the East Branch bridge, 1½ hours, 480-foot climb

The Siamese Ponds are 2.5 miles west of the hikers' bridge described in sections 18 and 89. Day hikers can make the walk in an hour; backpackers will find the 480-foot climb seems higher than it should, especially coming at the end of either the 7.2-mile walk from the north at Thirteenth Lake or the 4.2-mile walk from the south at NY 8. If you are carrying a full pack do not be surprised if the trek from the bridge to the ponds takes two hours. If you tire, there is an especially pretty place to stop and rest where the trail crosses the Siamese Ponds outlet.

The ponds are a symbol of remote wilderness, but it is a rare summer weekend when there are not at least three groups of campers on its shores, and in midweek it is unusual if there is only one group. Perhaps it is for that reason that several campers have expressed disappointment in their visit to the ponds.

Not too many years ago, Frank Warren, a guide, had a cabin on the ponds with rustic accommodations for fishermen and hunters, but this service, of course, is gone. However, the Unit Management Plan is recommending that a modern guide service which uses horse and carts to outfit hunting groups be allowed to use the trails in fall.

The first good campsite you will come to is near the trail, 200 yards before the first pond. If you want to camp on the more secluded north shore of the main pond, bushwhack the east shore or look for informal paths heading north from the trail. The easiest route is to leave the trail 0.5 mile west of the outlet crossing, before reaching the height-of-land. Circle around the small hill, walking generally northwest toward the pond. There are campsites on the shore of the upper, smaller pond; you can often find a rowboat on the first pond, but if you count on it for transportation to reach the upper pond, it is sure to be in use. Most groups of campers carry inflatable boats, an excellent way to explore and fish. Both ponds have been stocked with brook trout. You will find sandy beaches and very good swimming among the boulder- and birch-lined shores. However, if you pick a spot with a muddy shore, you are likely to find leeches.

There is a path around the south and west sides of the lower pond, which you can follow part of the way around to the upper pond, though the walk on the west becomes something of a bushwhack. There are also signs of an old tote road heading east from the northern lobe of the lower pond.

Cross-country skiers who want to try the Siamese Ponds Trail should note the hill on the trip out. The grade and the sharp turns make the descent difficult, and skiing down it should be attempted by expert wilderness skiers only.

20 Curtis Clearing

Moderate bushwhack, fishing, campsites

One way to leave the beaten path of the Siamese Ponds/East Branch Sacandaga Trail is to head for Curtis Clearing. Sportsmen say the fishing is good in Curtis Brook, but hikers almost never venture that way.

The old road is still visible and makes a good wilderness route. It is not marked and cleared so you will have to have a practiced eye to follow its partially overgrown track. Walk north on the East Branch Sacandaga Trail (section 18), almost to the Burnt Shanty Clearing, which is approximately 1 mile (thirty minutes walking) beyond the bridge over Diamond Brook. The road to Curtis Clearing heads west just past a large twin yellow birch and an old section of corduroy on the trail. If you miss it, walk to Burnt Shanty Clearing and then retrace your steps between 150 and 200 yards. Several blazed saplings also give clues to where it cuts off.

When you find it, follow it to the East Branch, which is shallow at this point and can be forded. There are cables located near a second ford, just downstream.

After following the road west from the river for ten minutes you will cross a small unnamed brook. Beyond, there is a swamp on the left and a ridge on the right with several good camping spots. Less than fifteen minutes of walking past the brook will bring you to a small clearing where the road seems to disappear. Walk straight through the clearing to pick up the road on the opposite side. For the next ten minutes you will be walking through a large stand of small spruce and balsam. Then you will reach Curtis Brook.

There are several good camping spots along the brook. After walking five more minutes you will cross the brook just below an old, very large beaver meadow. A clearing to the left is full of trash, unfortunately. The roadway ascends a small hill and within another ten minutes, you should reach an old clearing which has now become so overgrown that there are no longer views to the north. In fact, it is not easy to find a clear spot to camp. Two other old clearings, also filling in, stretch out to the west. There are apple trees, rock piles, and depressions that might be cellars, all parts of one of the Curtis farms. The road ends at the remains of an abandoned hunting camp west of the clearings.

The round-trip walk from NY 8 is over 8 miles and can be made in five and a half to six hours. If you want to try a camping expedition where there is little chance of meeting anyone else, this trek is ideal. The 1.2-mile-long abandoned road will take you a long way from civilization.

21 Western Cliffs on Eleventh Mountain
Easy bushwhack, excellent views

There are few places from which to view the interior wilderness valley of the East Branch of the Sacandaga, and of that small number the cliffs on the western face of Eleventh Mountain offer the most accessible perch. There is no path to them, but the bushwhack is easy to navigate and, with a little common sense, a safe route can be found to the cliff tops.

The cliffs are 600 feet above NY 8, but the first 200 feet can be accomplished in an easy fifteen-minute walk along the Siamese Ponds/East Branch Sacandaga Trail (section 18) to the saddle on the shoulder of Eleventh Mountain. The last 400 feet are attained in less than 0.3 mile, in a steep scramble up the mountain.

The best place to begin the steep bushwhacking ascent is 100 yards beyond the height-of-land on the trail. Here an old blaze (slash) on a beech tree marks the edge of a ferny, wet area and the closest approach to the cliffs. Pick a route that is approximately 40 degrees magnetic. This leads to the gentlest traverse of the cliff face and the easiest way around the small ledges. Generally wind up the benches on top of the ledges, climbing where it is easiest, which means sometimes almost straight up the smaller ledges.

You will reach the top of the shoulder of Eleventh Mountain south of the steepest and tallest ledges, which develop into a ring of cliffs that slope down to the north as they wrap around the mountain. Walk in either direction along the top of the ring of cliffs. There are many vantage points and the panorama is astonishing.

From the most southerly vantage on this knob, the valley of the East Branch beside NY 8 is visible. You can spot Hamilton Mountain in the distant west and the summit of Black Mountain looming in the southwest beyond Square Falls and Little Hopkins mountains.

From the area near the center of the ring of cliffs, a little north of your ascent, Big Hopkins, South Pond, and Horseshoe mountains are all visible to the west. Northwest of that trio, the cone shape of Humphrey Mountain is obvious, and beyond Humphrey the peaks and cliffs of Snowy Mountain mark the distant edge of Indian Lake. Squaw Mountain stands out to the north of Humphrey. Seven miles northwest across the East Branch valley, Puffer Mountain, with its exciting cliffs, and Bullhead, with its distinctive rock knob, mark the northern extent of the view. Those cliffs you see on Puffer are between 400 and 500 feet tall and range for over 0.5 mile on the mountain's southeast face; the tops and most of the escarpment are well hidden by a heavy cover of spruce.

The distant views are not improved by descending to the ledges on the north, though from there the cliffs on Diamond Mountain are very close. In summer, this perch on Eleventh Mountain is great for watching soaring hawks and otherwise extending the two or three hours needed to climb the cliffs into a beautiful day's adventure.

To return, retrace your steps as carefully as possible. If you are not careful you could encounter a ridge that leads to cliffs too high to descend further, while reclimbing the same ridge would be nearly impossible. Scout carefully ahead.

View from Eleventh Mountain

22 Eastern Cliffs and Waterfall on Eleventh Mountain
Easy bushwhack, intermittent waterfall

The view from the eastern cliffs on Eleventh Mountain may not be as spectacular as those from some other mountains north of NY 8, but the climb to them is by far the easiest, and here there is no river to cross.

The cliffs are visible from NY 8 about halfway between the Siamese Ponds trailhead and Bakers Mills. Even though the shortest route to the cliffs crosses some private land, it is possible to begin the walk on public land. The state has purchased a wooded lot to the east of the Straight Farm and access to the cliffs begins at the edge of these woods. Pick a compass route that will take you to the east of the cliffs. The scoot up the mountain is so easy that a compass is not essential, but have one with you to be sure you do not get lost. From the eastern corner of the Straight Farm at the edge of the woods, the route is toward magnetic north. Walk along the eastern edge of the farm, against second-growth woods. You may find an old road through scrubby new growth to a gravel pit. Walking is easy through the abandoned fields, where occasional blackberry patches and small evergreens are beginning to grow.

As the route becomes steep, you will see the remnants of a road that used to lead through a sugarbush. Walking beneath the huge maples is open and easy. The yellow paint spotted on the tree trunks indicates the boundary of state land. Already you will find a few small ledges with good views, hints of what is to come.

Walk to the east of the highest ledge to get around it and up to the summit ridge. Here you will find a footpath, slightly brushed out. The summit is covered with dense thickets of spruce and hemlock and walking through them is very rough except on the informal paths.

From the first cliff top you encounter while walking west along the ridge there is a fantastic view of Crane and Huckleberry mountains and glimpses of the range of mountains past the Hudson to the east. Kettle is the huge, heavily wooded mountain to the south and west and Mount Blue looms behind it.

Use the rudimentary paths to continue along and up the ridge, west, to the top of the cliffs. If you arrive in summer, it will take a bit of imagination to see the waterfall that can spill over the cliff. An intermittent stream drains a small, thickly wooded swamp on the shoulder of Eleventh Mountain. In spring that stream pours a silvery thread down the bare rock, creating a lovely waterfall that can be seen from NY 8. In dry times, only the precipitous rock slide, nearly 100 feet tall, marks the location.

Be careful in wet weather; mosses at the top of the falls can be slippery. Even in dry weather do not venture too near the top of the falls. The slope is deceptive and the bottom is not visible from a safe vantage point.

In dry weather you can follow the stream bed toward the swamp. The layers of rock resemble a poured cement walkway. Beyond the swamp, there is a range of small hills across the summit, none with views and all covered with the most dense thickets of small balsam. Even the scattering of huge boulders and rock ledges do not compensate for the difficult terrain. Many of the *dryopteris* ferns found on the summit are the species *campyloptera*, the mountain wood fern, which is rarely found in the southern Adirondacks.

The 800-foot climb to the cliff top from the farm requires less than an hour. The descent takes even less time. On the return, be careful to walk all the way east along the ridge before beginning the descent to avoid the cliffs and steepest ledges. It is best, on this mountain, to retrace your ascent as carefully as possible.

23 Second Pond

Path, fishing, picnic sites, campsites, cross-country skiing

Second Pond is favored by its location in the valley west of Gore and Height of Land mountains. The setting is perfect, as is the length of path to reach it: short enough for a one-day trip but long enough to be in remote wilderness.

The access to Second Pond is from Chatiemac Road, 0.5 mile west of Sodom on the north side of NY 8. The road ends at Chatiemac Lake, a private lake with cottages and a clubhouse. The state has recently acquired a large tract of land that includes all but the lake and its immediate shores, adding it to the Siamese Ponds Wilderness.

The path to Second Pond starts from the right side of Chatiemac Road, 2.3 miles from NY 8, just before the "Keep out—Private" sign. It begins as a good, but unmarked path that avoids all the private land. Because it is such a level, easy route, it should be good for cross-country skiing and snowshoeing, except that it is unmarked and hard to follow in winter. It also has received little maintenance in recent years, leaving a number of deadfalls across the trail.

The path heads north from Chatiemac Road and you soon reach the outlet of Chatiemac Lake, which you cross on the rocks below a beaver dam. Immediately before the outlet, there is a footpath off to the right which you might want to follow to a little marsh made by the flow of Black Mountain Brook. It is a handsome spot with Gore Mountain rising to the north across the lovely flow.

Retracing your steps and crossing the outlet, you start a gradual climb through very open woods with a high canopy of tall straight trees and a low understory. The path follows a ridge that appears to be an esker, open and with ferns and a through-the-trees view of a marsh off to the right. After about twenty minutes of going uphill you will see large glacial erratics, especially impressive on the right.

As the path contours around the east side of Height of Land Mountain, you can look down into the valley of Black Mountain Brook on the right. After twenty-five minutes, you are still going up, heading now almost west. The path deteriorates as the understory has grown up. Witch hobble and thickets grown over the path around downed beech trees would make this difficult to follow, especially in winter, but someone has put red paint on just enough trees to mark the continuing way. In summer those thickets around the path are solid stands of horse nettles—wear long pants!

As the path approaches a height-of-land, after about a forty-minute walk, it crosses a drainage, making a very acute angle with what appears to be a draw. The path continues west, descending gently, then contouring, with little ups and downs. Beyond, the path crosses a second drainage, this one coming from the steeper slopes to the left of the path. Beyond the second, the path continues west then gradually turns to the north to round a small hill which lies on the southeast shore of the pond. The route is now downhill, swinging from north through northeast as it approaches the pond. After about an hour and a half of walking, you will make the final descent to a point about midway along the pond's south shore.

At the shore you will find a clearing beneath tall evergreens and a fire ring with space for several tents. Remnants of wooden rowboats are now strewn about in pieces. Second Pond is stocked with trout, but it is difficult to fish it without a boat as there are many snags near the shore. The shore is heavily wooded and ringed with sweet gale and difficult to walk around.

The pond nestles under part of Gore Mountain and is quite picturesque. The main summit of Gore is just out of sight around to the right from the shore at the end of the path. The 2.7-mile walk is appropriate for family picnics, short camping trips, and fishing, if you carry an inflatable raft. The colors are especially impressive for a fall walk.

24 Bog Meadow and Second Pond Brook

Path, old road, cross-country skiing, picnic sites, campsites

Walk to Bog Meadow in the fall when the leaves are nearly off; color and distant views will be exceptional for such a level route. In winter, ski the old road bed that serves as the route for most of the path—it is a fantastic run that leads 4 miles through wilderness to scenic meadows. And if you really want an off-the-beaten path for a winter ski-touring trip, use this route together with the path to Second Pond (section 23) and a course down the outlet of Second Pond. The loop, best run counterclockwise, would give an expert a full day of hard skiing. Since none of the way is marked, note that winter navigation can be difficult. Also, there has been no maintenance on the route in recent years, and there is currently quite a bit of blowdown. Beavers have been at work on many streams, so summer flooding is possible.

Except in winter, the abandoned road to Bog Meadow makes a fairly obvious route. Hunters use horse and wagon to haul gear along it for fall hunting trips, so downed trees have been cleared from the beginning of the route. To find this old logging road, leave NY 8 at Bakers Mills and drive 1.5 miles north on Edwards Hill Road. Just beyond a Swiss-type chalet and a green and white house on the left—and just before a wetland—you will see a narrow roadway with crushed stone base and a sign, "Fogarty." The shoulders of the paved road are wide enough here for parking. When you stop, look back south to enjoy the beautiful view of Crane Mountain; you are standing below the heavily wooded summit of Eleventh Mountain to the west. At the end of this paved road there is a private camp of special interest to hikers: it is the place where Howard Zahniser drafted the Federal Wilderness Act.

Walk west along the private road marked Fogarty and as their driveway forks right, stay straight on the old logging road. This is private property for the first 0.5 mile and no motorized vehicles are allowed. In ten minutes you come to a fork with a private road going off to the left; there is a chain across it which may be down in summer. Go right, up the hill. As the logging road ascends the shoulder of Eleventh Mountain, you pass through scrub forest and low brush and weeds. In the fall the views of the valley spread out below you. Going west of north, you enter a second-growth spruce woods.

After about twelve minutes of hiking, just over 0.5 mile, you reach the state land boundary sign which is the beginning of the Siamese Ponds

Gilead

Rabbit
Pond

The Vly

North Creek
Reservoir

Pete Gay
Mtn

Roaring

Brook

otheration
Pond

Halfway

Tailings

Bartons
Mine

Open Pit
Mine

GORE MTN

Upper Dam
Pond

3583 Lookout Tower

Straight

Black Mtn Bk

Brook

Second
Pond

(23)

Height of Land
Mtn

Ward
Hill

Mud
Pond

Chatiemac
Lake

Round
Pond

Chatiemac

Brook

Round Pond

Brook

(24)

Bog Meadow

Edwards
Hill

Windover
Lake

Sodon

Baker

H   N   S   B   U   R   G

(25)

District Sch
No 7

Edwards
Hill

BM
1532

BM
1584

Morehouse

Bakers
Mills

E L E V E N T H   M O U N T A I N

(22)

BM

Map III Sections 18-25, 69, 71, 74 and 85-90
Based on USGS 15'
Thirteenth Lake Quadrangle

Creek

(21)

N

Path
Trail
Bushwhack
Road
Cliffs

0   1 mile

Second Pond Flow

Wilderness Area. There is a No Motorized Vehicles sign. At this point a path comes in from the right, from Edwards Hill Road, but do not try to use it. You continue making a gentle ascent; in the summer this section is loaded with horse nettles, so wear long pants. The breadth of the path makes this an excellent cross-country ski trail. After twenty minutes of hiking, you reach a corduroy road in a water course and after this there is a fork; keep right, in fact the rule for following this unmarked route is to keep right always, until the Mud Lake fork.

After hiking for twenty-five minutes, while going uphill, you may see a red tie on a tree and another left fork. Stay right here; the left fork is a hunters' path which goes along Diamond Brook. Past this fork, you descend a gentle slope to Diamond Brook, which is very small at this point. In the next five minutes you will walk through spruce woods with two small glacial erratics on the right, one split. Notice as the land on the left begins to drop away. The trail in this evergreen-covered section is more obviously an old wagon road.

After about a fifty-five-minute walk, as you notice the gully on the left or south really begin to deepen, you should notice a path heading right. It goes to Mud Pond and a hunters' camp and then on to Second Pond, but it is difficult to follow past the camp. As you take the left fork, look across the ravine to the extensive number of dead spruce on the hillside. Dead spruce are appearing in large numbers throughout the Adirondacks, probably the result of acid rain that has stressed the trees and made them susceptible to drought and disease.

The old road then drops down toward Round Pond Brook. In about fifteen minutes it bottoms out and there is a left fork which goes up a grade to a hunters' camping site. Take the right fork which then contours around the bottom of the hillside, heading southwest. The large beaver meadow visible through the trees to the left is Bog Meadow. The small stream feeding it comes in from the right—you cross it after about an hour's walk. Bog Meadow stretches off to the left, a large, grassy vly about three hundred yards in diameter. On the left there is an informal campsite with an old stove, but the brook is sluggish and this is not a choice place to camp.

The path continues around the right side of the meadow and crosses the brook again. Even in a dry year, this is a wet area with ferns, sphagnum, slippery rocks, and many nettles. A little over ten minutes after crossing the brook the second time, the path begins to descend with lower ground falling away to the right. A little over twenty minutes after the second crossing there is a not-too-easy-to-spot V in the trail. The left fork is currently the more obvious as it is a freshly cleared section of the old road which once led to a logging camp and now leads to a hunters' camp. It offers a half-hour round-trip walk through the woods—not very exciting, but excellent for cross-country skiing.

The right fork is a narrow path down the hill. In two or three minutes you will see an old stove in a clearing off to the left. Go past the stove and continue west for about five minutes, then turn north where you have to push through spruce to find a way into the long, grassy meadow which surrounds Second Pond Brook. Long ago, beavers dammed the brook and this broad, natural field is the result. You can picnic on the remains of the old beaver dam and, if you are lucky, hear the sharp cry of a broad-winged hawk from the towering pines across the vly to the north. The best part of this 4-mile, two-and-a-half-hour hike is this series of meadows at the end. Any hiker will enjoy this path along the old road which was built to haul out logs and hemlock bark. The recent clearing will make it delightful for cross-country skiers, who can easily glide across the meadows at the end.

25 Diamond Brook
Easy bushwhack, fishing

Diamond Brook, which drains a shallow valley into the East Branch of the Sacandaga, substitutes for the more traditional compass heading on an easy bushwhack north of Eleventh Mountain. You reach the brook by walking northwest for 1.5 miles on the Siamese Ponds/East Branch Sacandaga Trail (section 18). A fairly level, unspectacular, and occasionally hard walk upstream will then take you to the path of section 24 and eventually to Edwards Hill Road. Because it is doubtful you would want to walk the brook in both directions, it would be better to have a car parked on Edwards Hill Road, at the head of the path to Bog Meadows (section 24) where you emerge. Typical Adirondack undergrowth and blowdowns, mostly beech, contribute to the difficulty of bushwhacking along the stream. The slight grade from the East Branch to the brook's headwaters means there are no falls and no large pools to enhance the stream, which is frequented by fishermen.

Diamond Mountain shows clearly on the left as you start up the brook, and you will find a few fishermen's footpaths on the south bank. The brook flows down through forests of hemlock and other evergreens in the first mile, and there are blowdowns on both sides. Fortunately, the brook is generally shallow enough so you can cross from side to side to take advantage of the easiest walking. One mile upstream the brook divides around a small island, 1 mile farther a huge downed pine provides a sturdy bridge, and 2.5 miles beyond that there is an old beaver flow. Walking around the south side of it will bring you to a hunters' camp on a small rise. The easiest route for finishing the walk is along the hunters' path to this camp from Edwards Hill Road (section 24).

After walking that path for 0.5 mile, you will merge with the path from Bog Meadows, which comes in from the left, or northwest. As you turn right, downhill, you can see the north shoulder of Eleventh Mountain on your right. From this point on you follow the logging road described in section 24. State land ends before you reach a field near the road's end. The complete through trek is 6.7 miles long and takes about five hours.

Along the Main Branch of the Sacandaga

THE MAIN BRANCH of the Sacandaga River serves as one of the southern boundaries for the areas covered in this guide. It is the outlet of Lake Pleasant and begins near Speculator by flowing northeast. It is joined almost immediately by the Kunjamuk, which drains the large valley to the northeast. East of the confluence, the Sacandaga heads south and courses through a narrow valley, roughly parallel to NY 8/30. Even though some of the adjacent lands belong to International Paper Company, only one of the excursions described requires a permit (see section 30).

The Sacandaga River is bordered on the east by Old Route 30, which used to loop east from the newer NY 8/30 highway. Because the southern bridge over the Sacandaga that connected the two roads is closed and not scheduled to be rebuilt, the only connection to Old Route 30 is 7 miles north of the southern intersection of NY 8 and 30. The connection is 3 miles south of the northern intersection of NY 8 and 30 in Speculator.

Old Route 30 is now a quiet dead-end road, 3.6 miles long, leading to several picnic sites. A new hydroelectric project on the Sacandaga near the northern end of the road in the vicinity of Christine Falls has closed all public access to the area around those falls, hence Christine Falls has been omitted from this guide.

26 Auger Falls/West Side
Picnic site, short trail, footpaths, boat launch
1-mile loop, ½ hour, minimal vertical rise

A remote, almost wilderness trek to the east side of Auger Falls is described in section 2. A very short, much traveled trail leads from NY 8/30 to the west side of the falls, which are the largest on the main branch of the Sacandaga River. That trail begins near a turnout on NY 8/30 by a sign for an International Paper Company picnic site for which no IP permit is

required. The sign does not indicate that picnic facilities are present, just that no camping is allowed on company property. The falls and access to them are on land acquired by the state with the assistance of the Nature Conservancy.

The marked turnout is 1.5 miles north of the NY 8 bridge over the Sacandaga, on the east side of NY 8/30. The turnout leads immediately to a short, 0.2-mile stretch of dirt road that parallels the highway. On the north it ends in a picnic area beside the still waters of Auger Flats, upstream from the falls. The trail to the falls begins at the southern end of the short road.

Recently marked by the state, the trail is 0.3 mile long. Yellow disks delineate the principal route to the falls, although several informal paths also branch out from it, leading to different vantage points on the cliffs above the falls and to a pool below them. None are more than a couple hundred feet long and you will want to explore them all.

Be careful! It is always damp and slippery beside the falls, and it is especially dangerous in spring when the whole gorge is misted with its spray. The rock slides beside the falls are gouged with potholes; one that is visible in late summer and fall is four feet deep. Some have rocks in them that continue to churn and grind them deeper. Auger Falls is actually a series of small steps, and it is frustrating that the entire chute of water is not visible from any safe vantage point.

At the north end of the falls you can either return via the yellow-marked trail or continue north and west on a footpath that is unmarked but nonetheless clear and easy to follow. The path curves beside the river, past the rapids, and west to the northern end of the picnic access road by Auger Flats (see section 27).

The entire loop walk that starts at the picnic area, goes south to the trail, heads east to the falls, then returns by the unmarked path, can be walked in a half hour, but you need much more time because I doubt you will find a prettier walk of comparable length anywhere in the Adirondacks. It is amazing how much there is to see. If you do stop here, be sure to bring your camera.

27 Auger Flats
Short canoe trip

Just upstream of Auger Falls, the Sacandaga broadens into a smooth-flowing waterway. In fact, much of the year, the water moves so slowly that it is impossible to imagine the fury of this same river as it is funneled into the narrow chasm that creates the falls downstream. Auger Flats, as this stretch of water is called, makes such a short canoe trip that you may want to combine it with a walk to Auger Falls (section 26).

Launch your canoe at the north end of the picnic access road where you turn off NY 8/30 to reach the falls. Do not paddle downstream toward the rapids; instead head upstream through the flowed lands. Here the Sacandaga winds through a stand of magnificent silver maples that overhang the waterway and are repeated in images in the still water.

It is possible to paddle your canoe upriver for some 1.5 miles alongside NY 30, although the bends and twists of the river make the distance much longer. Where the river weaves away from the road into dense woods, you will feel quite remote from civilization. Birding along the stream is fantastic. It is a favorite spot for rose-breasted grosbeaks, who nest low in trees almost at the water's edge.

28 Escarpment on Macomber Mountain
Moderate bushwhack, snowshoeing

As you drive north along NY 8/30 past Auger Flats on the Sacandaga, notice the sheer rock face of the mountain to the east. The southern slopes of the low shoulder of Macomber Mountain were burned in the early sixties, exposing the rock and opening a great and accessible view.

There is no trail to the exposed escarpment, so a bushwhack is necessary to take in the views. The easiest access begins from the sand pits adjacent to Old Route 30 that are east of the closed bridge. To reach the sand pits, drive 3.6 miles south on Old Route 30 to its present terminus or walk across the bridge (it is closed only to vehicles), which is 2 miles north of the Auger Falls Picnic area.

The cliffs and most of the route to them are on state land, but you will need a permit to cross International Paper Company's land adjacent to Old Route 30. See section 30 for permit information.

Auger Falls

The most direct route is straight up the mountain from the sand pit, south of a small stream that cuts through the pit area, 200 yards south of the end of the road. A compass heading of 105 degrees magnetic will take you to the escarpment in an hour and ten minutes, but you will have to fight through brambles and scrub growth on the burned-over southwestern face of the hillside first. Big charred trees and stumps ring the lower level, while thick blackberries and new growth choke the top.

Although that route is most direct, for those comfortable with cross-country routes, there is a better way. The fires did not scar the hill behind the cliffs, so walking there is easier. Walk east from the sand pits to pick up a logging road and a branch of the stream that flows from Macomber. Follow all the right forks in the stream up the hill. The route will take you to a draw north of the escarpment. Climb through the top of the draw to the ridge. From the ridge, crossing the summit south to open rock is easy because there are big trees and relatively easy walking across the top.

At its highest, the escarpment is a steep slide nearly 300 feet long. It wraps around the mountain for about a quarter mile, offering views through over 200 degrees. From the top, the broad expanse of the Sacandaga valley stretches out at your feet. There are views of Speculator, Hamilton, Round, and Dunham mountains to the west. On the eastern horizon you will spot Crane Mountain and Mount Blue and all the hills that rim NY 8 and the East Branch of the Sacandaga.

Try this route as a winter snowshoe trek. The mountain is not too steep for winter climbing, and the escarpment is one of the few cliffs in this guide that can be reached safely in winter. Many others involve crossing dangerous streams and rivers. However, you should check to see whether the winds that whip down the Sacandaga valley have left a dangerous coating of ice on the open areas before venturing across the summit, and, of course, keep back from the top of the escarpment.

Two hours for the round trip is adequate in both summer and winter. The escarpment is less than a mile from NY 8.

29 Austin Falls
Picnic site, waterfalls

To reach the area of Austin Falls, drive south on Old Route 30 for almost 3 miles. International Paper Company has designated a picnic site beside the Sacandaga at this point. Upstream, the Sacandaga rushes through a long slide that is punctuated with several small falls and deep chutes. The chute is called Austin Falls.

The handsome rock base of the falls is elegantly sculptured by the water. In one place, smooth pink rock has been worn into small pink peaks that resemble standing waves or stiffly beaten egg whites.

The chute's accessibility makes it a favorite with photographers and picnickers. The gorge is not deep and dangerous, but the banks are slippery nevertheless. On one stop here, it was a shock to see a skindiver plunging into one of the deepest pools to retrieve an expensive camera that had been swept into the whirlpool when its owner ventured too close. The torrent of water from the spring melt is incredible.

The Kunjamuk

ONE OF THIS region's major valleys stretches north 12 miles from Speculator to Kunjamuk Mountain. The valley is broad and flat, and the river that drains it, the Kunjamuk, drops less than 200 feet from its major sources to its terminus at the Sacandaga River. The origin of the name Kunjamuk is unexplained, but the names of the mountains and streams near it compose a natural description of the area. On the south, Rift Hill borders the first major rifts of the Sacandaga River; Oak, Pine, and Mossy mountains all have the features their names suggest; Poplar Hill is not far from an area where today there are stands of large poplar; Dug Mountain has its old mine; Cave Hill has the requisite cave; and Elm Lake on the Kunjamuk has the remnants of one of the larger northern elm forests.

The long flat valley of the Kunjamuk is a sandy plain which was once the bottom of a glacial lake. Little wonder that the first roads north to Indian Lake village passed through it and its extension, the Kings Flow-Round Pond outlet valley on the north. Imagine finding a valley system anywhere in the eastern Adirondacks where the total change in elevation over 20 miles is less than 300 feet. Only the shorter Thirteenth Lake and East Branch Sacandaga valleys to the east could provide a route for a comparable road system.

The first roads were pushed north from Speculator toward Elm Lake in 1815. One of the nineteenth century's dreamers even proposed that a railroad, the Schenectady and Ogdensburg, cross the Sacandaga near Wells and head north through the Kunjamuk and Kings Flow valleys to Indian Lake. The old road today is just one of the area's many long, flat hiking routes.

It is not only the geographical features that gave rise to the routes around the Kunjamuk. International Paper Company has holdings which encompass almost all of the Kunjamuk valley, and its system of logging roads honeycombs the diamond-shaped tract of land, which is six miles on a side. These roads provide a unique access system for sportsmen. The story of how the entire section, Township Nine, came to belong to International Paper Company is fascinating.

All of the International Paper Company lands on both sides of the Kunjamuk were once owned by the Rhinelander family. Frederick Rhinelander purchased Township Nine of the Totten and Crossfield patent in the late 1700s. In 1815, his nephew, Philip Rhinelander, Jr., began construction of an elegant mansion on Elm Lake, through which the Kunjamuk flows. He gradually acquired more land, specifically around Speculator. He managed the family's property as a farm, importing slaves and servants to clear the land and tame the wilderness.

Exotic mahogany paneling and furniture graced the mansion's large rooms. Orchards and flower gardens replaced the native forests. Philip increased the family's fortunes with his gristmills and sawmills and the stock he pastured on the many cleared fields. He had a road built from Lake Pleasant to his mansion, and then north beside the Kunjamuk.

Although Philip Rhinelander was a leader in the Lake Pleasant community, his private life gave rise to rumors and gossip. His insane jealousy was supposed to have driven him to keep his beautiful young wife a prisoner in the mansion. Her death in 1818 increased the speculation. In 1823, Philip was "seized with paralysis" and left for New York City.

He had made little impression on the wilderness, for Spafford's *Gazetteer* of 1824 described the community of Elm Lake as "a savage wilderness, of which no more need be said, than, that for ages yet to come, it will probably remain such."

Caretakers managed the estate but no one lived in the boarded-up mansion where apparitions eventually convinced all who worked there that the house was haunted. Around 1875, the building burned. The parcel of land remained intact and later almost all of Township Nine was sold to International Paper Company.

30   Permits for Access to International Paper Company Lands

Much of International Paper Company's tract, the Speculator Tree Farm, which encompasses the Kunjamuk, is now open by permit only. Permits, ranging from day use to seasonal use, can be obtained from the company's Speculator Woodlands Office on Old Route 30 just south of Speculator or from several merchants in Speculator. The nominal day use fee of $3.00 may be raised in 1990. The only exceptions to the permit requirements are for those canoeing to Elm Lake or driving East Road, which is a town road, to reach state lands.

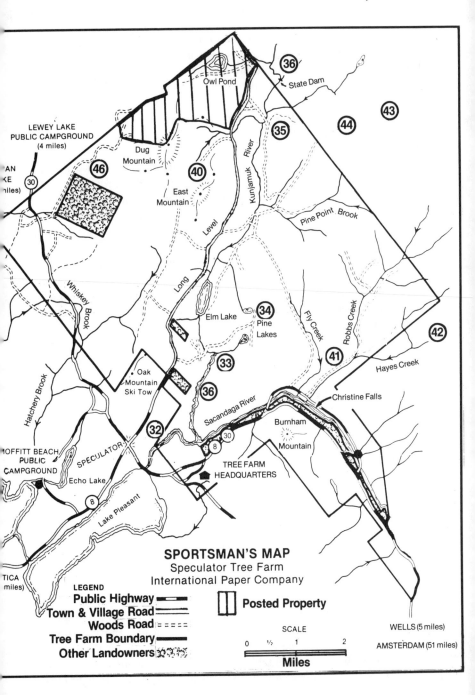

LEWEY LAKE
PUBLIC CAMPGROUND
(4 miles)

State Dam

Owl Pond

Dug
Mountain

East
Mountain

Kunjamuk River

Pine Point Brook

Long Level

Elm Lake

Pine Lakes

Fly Creek

Robbs Creek

Hayes Creek

Oak
Mountain
Ski Tow

Sacandaga River

Christine Falls

Whiskey Brook

Hatchery Brook

SPECULATOR

Echo Lake

Lake Pleasant

MOFFITT BEACH
PUBLIC
CAMPGROUND

TREE FARM
HEADQUARTERS

Burnham
Mountain

UTICA
(miles)

SPORTSMAN'S MAP
Speculator Tree Farm
International Paper Company

LEGEND
Public Highway
Town & Village Road
Woods Road
Tree Farm Boundary
Other Landowners

Posted Property

SCALE
0   ½   1   2

Miles

WELLS (5 miles)

AMSTERDAM (51 miles)

The change in IP's policy is a result of the economics of logging. Taxes are sufficiently high so that no one seems to make a profit from land just by logging it. Recreation is becoming an increasingly important source of revenue for the timber industry. Many paper companies have granted exclusive leases that eliminate public access. At present, there are only two exclusive leases in this tract, one in the vicinity of Owl Pond and another at the end of Whitaker Lake Road. The latter covers all of the north face of Dug Mountain.

You will need a permit to drive all of the roads in the IP tract with the exception of East Road, a town road. The beginning of that road, which is north of Speculator, is in pretty bad shape and only usable by four-wheel-drive vehicles. Because IP has been actively logging tracts east of the Kunjamuk, the Fly Creek Road is a better alternate beginning as far as the Long Level Bridge.

Some of the logging roads are the best for walking, as they are great for watching birds and butterflies and picking blackberries and raspberries in season. In addition to the many opportunities for sportsmen in the tract, one of the greatest benefits of the road system is the unique access it provides to the deep interior wilderness of the Siamese Ponds area. In spite of the fact that the woods are logged and disturbed, the accesses are remarkably clean and free of litter. Sections 32 through 47 describe the roads and the adventures accessible from them.

No camping, fires, or ATVs are permitted on International Paper Company's Speculator Tree Farm.

31 The Lower Kunjamuk in Winter

Cross-country ski trail
5 miles, 1½ hours, minimal vertical rise

A cross-country ski trail has been designed and laid out on lands leased from International Paper Company. The trail, with a long and short loop and an extension to the Kunjamuk Cave (section 33), is groomed by the village of Speculator. It intertwines the existing complex of snowmobile trails that follow old logging roads in the area. Its only disadvantage is that high water conditions on the Kunjamuk can flood the portions that are in the flood plain of the river. Maps are available locally, and you should consult one to be sure you have the most recent details for the system.

The Kunjamuk route is suitable for those with moderate cross-country skiing experience. The five-mile loop to the caves, marked with light blue, diamond-shaped disks, begins at the head of the parking area behind the fire house on NY 8/30, south of their Speculator intersection. From here it leads northeast along the flood plain of the Sacandaga, paralleling the river. In half a mile it crosses a snowmobile trail and a spur of the ski trail forks left to East Road. For nearly a mile, the ski trail parallels a snowmobile trail which it crosses just before the ski trail splits to form either the long or short loops.

For the trip to the cave, keep left, a route which leads northeast over a small knob, then down through a saddle on the north side of the hill, which rises about 80 feet from the flood plain. The short loop forks right, but stay straight, descending to a tree plantation where the route joins a level logging road, which is the road access to the cave described in section 33. Turn right, south, and ski 0.4 mile to the bridge over the Kunjamuk. A 0.2-mile trek east of the bridge leads to the cave.

To complete the long loop, return from the cave to the bridge, cross it, and ski the level route beside the Kunjamuk. Be sure the flood plain is frozen before attempting this section, for you may have to ski around clumps of alders that occasionally grow quite close to open water. The short loop trail is a right fork if you are headed south along the Kunjamuk. Your route will rejoin the Sacandaga and, shortly beyond, complete the loop to retrace the mile stretch back to the parking area.

During the week, you can enjoy skiing the snowmobile trails which will also take you to the Kunjamuk Bridge. On weekends, the noise from those trails sometimes detracts from the skiing. The trip to the cave and back, including a picnic on the way, is less than four hours, even if you ski all the loops.

32 Roads in the Kunjamuk Tract
Chart to logging roads

The logging roads that lace International Paper Company's Speculator Tree Farm can seem like a maze. The map on page 81 shows those roads accessible to four-wheel-drive vehicles, with a recommended speed of 15 miles per hour. Use this map as a guide to the trailheads and canoe accesses of sections 33 through 44. Note particularly that IP no longer permits the public to use ATVs on these roads.

The names of the roads along the Kunjamuk are as confusing as the network itself, and there are almost no road signs. East Road, which is the road east from Speculator's principal intersection, is the road on the *west*

side of the Kunjamuk. It is a town road and open to the public without a permit. However, the beginning of the road is in bad shape until you reach Long Level.

Because IP has been logging the portion of the tract east of the Kunjamuk extensively, the Fly Creek Road is now in excellent shape as far as the Long Level Bridge and is the best way to reach the northern part of East Road. You will need a permit to drive Fly Creek Road, which begins 2 miles south on Old Route 30. Northern Fly Creek Road and Upper Pine Ponds Road are strictly for four-wheel-drive vehicles. The Upper Bridge that connects Fly Creek Road with East Road still stands, but it is barred to vehicles. It is reached by a right turn less than a mile from the end of East Road.

There are outhouses in the gravel pits to the west of Long Level Bridge.

33 Kunjamuk Cave

Logging road, hiking, exploring

There is some speculation that the cave on the east side of Cave Hill at the lower end of the Kunjamuk valley is not natural. Perhaps someone dug it while prospecting for the silver and gold that were rumored to seam nearby mountains. Since silver was actually found in a mine on Dug Mountain, to the north across the Kunjamuk, it would not be surprising if this small cave was also carved out of the hillside.

However, the seams of shiny material in the cave's walls are calcite and the smooth face of its back and roof suggests that a geological explanation for its existence may be more logical. The entire Kunjamuk valley was a glacial lake; layers of very fine sand cover it today. Perhaps the cave was formed as a pothole worn in the rock of the side hill by glacial melt waters churning grindstones.

There are three ways to reach the Kunjamuk Cave. Perhaps the easiest is to paddle a canoe north from Speculator along the river (section 36) to the new footbridge constructed for the ski-touring trail. Leave your canoe and head up the path on the east side of the bridge to a small clearing. You are actually on a logging road, the right side of which traverses the clearing and heads south along the Kunjamuk. As you enter the clearing, walk straight across it, toward the hillside, to the northeast corner. Here pick up

Cliffs on Upper Pine Mountain from Fly Creek Road in Speculator Tree Farm

the logging road where it climbs and circles the saddle of a small hill before proceeding southeast to NY 30. The cave is 200 yards from the clearing on the left side of the road. A few light blue markers point the way, which is fortunate, as in summer weeds conceal the roads through the clearing.

Of course, you can also approach the cave by way of the ski-touring and nature trails described in section 31. Note that in summer the first mile north from the firehouse south of Speculator alongside the Kunjamuk is on low ground and may be wet and swampy. However, the trail is marked and features interpretive signs, which detail the importance of the flood plain, International Paper Company's forest management practices, and habitats of unusual plant and animal life in the area. The round trip by this route is 5 miles.

The third approach to the cave begins on East Road (section 32). In summer drive just over 1 mile northeast from Speculator on East Road, past Oak Mountain and the end of the macadam. The easiest directions from here are simply to take all right turns on roads that are passable to four-wheel-drive vehicles. (There are other turns from the road, the ski-touring trail being one of them.)

It is probably best to park just beyond the end of the macadam, and enjoy the birds and butterflies on the way to the cave. Turn right on Pine Lakes Road and walk 0.7 mile past the main road to a right fork in a plantation area and then 0.2 mile on that road to the river and footbridge. It is 0.2 mile and a five-minute walk beyond the bridge to the cave.

34 Pine Lakes
Logging road, picnic site

The Pine Lakes are a pair of very tiny, rather swampy lakes, not the most exciting of destinations. However, the walk to them is so lovely that this route is especially recommended for those who favor a dirt road for birding, berry-picking, and picnicking rather than a wilderness trail.

Access to the logging road is from East Road, out of Speculator (section 32). Pine Lakes Road is the first right on East Road past the end of the macadam. Either park at this corner and start your walk here or drive to the third right turn. (The first leads to Kunjamuk Cave, described in section 33.) The International Paper Company road is good to within a short distance, less than 0.2 mile, of the bridge over the Kunjamuk. If you choose to drive partway, turn down the third road on the right and park in the field near the intersection, off the road. The dirt road ahead and the bridge over the Kunjamuk are not passable except on foot.

Continue on Pine Lakes Road, walking generally northeast across the bridge. On a bright, sunny day, you will agree that this is one of the most delightful roads in International Paper Company's Kunjamuk Tract. Half an hour of walking will bring you to a T in the road, 1 mile from your start. The left fork leads in 0.3 mile, about a ten-minute walk, to a camp where a small path cuts down to a picnic spot on the northern Pine Lake, which is shallow and muddy and not suitable for swimming. Even the picnic spot may be muddy.

The right fork leads south along a logging road, where there is a turnoff to the southern Pine Lake. This lake is also a ten-minute, 0.3-mile walk from the junction. In summer you could miss it, so watch as the road curves a little east and a log blocks the way. About 100 feet short of the log, the turnoff, a nearly concealed path, bears downhill to the right, and brings you to a real bog, a nearly "dead" lake with sphagnum mats filling the shores and many typical bog plants.

35 Cliffs on Upper Pine Mountain
Easy bushwhack, excellent views

From the Upper Bridge over the Kunjamuk (section 32) you can see the cliffs on Upper Pine Mountain to the east. Rising between 300 and 400 feet above the valley flood plain, they are not difficult to reach. A climb traversing the face of the mountain offers several interesting vantage points.

Because you cannot drive along the northern Fly Creek Road, use northern East Road and turn east from it 2 miles north of the Long Level intersection. This leads to the closed bridge over the Kunjamuk, which you can still walk across. Head east, then when the road turns south, start up Pine Mountain, bushwhacking southeast for the gentlest climb to the top of the cliffs. The first views are north along the Kunjamuk valley. From some points, quite a bit of the valley is visible; the mountains commanding the view west are Dug and East. Views to the south along the river are excellent. In less than one hour you will reach the uppermost of the cliffs, passing a half dozen other open spots on the way.

It is unfortunate that this short, rewarding climb is accessible only to those whose vehicles can take them over the back roads of the Kunjamuk Tract.

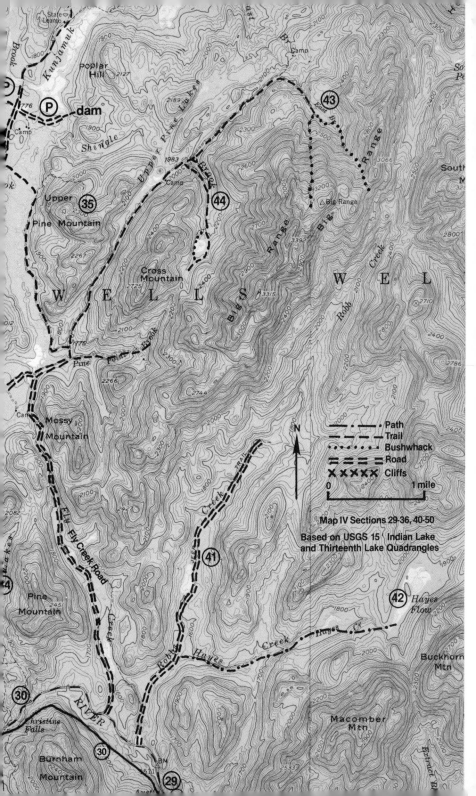

36 Canoeing the Kunjamuk

Only rarely as you canoe along the meandering and twisted course of the Kunjamuk will you feel you are in recently timbered and disturbed land. Thickets of alders, fields of marsh grass and reeds, and splashes of brilliantly colored wildflowers separate you from any logged areas. Attempting a two-day camping trip on the Kunjamuk is complicated by the fact you cannot camp on IP lands. Shallow water and snags make it almost impossible to canoe all the way north from Speculator to state lands in one day.

Upstream from the Long Level Bridge above Elm Lake, the river has been freed of many of the snags that have made travel there difficult in the past. However, this section is very shallow and often slow going. With this in mind, the simplest way to canoe the Kunjamuk may be a one-day trip to Elm Lake and back. For this no permit is required. The best way is to have someone drop you off at the Fish Barrier dam or the bridge just south of it.

SACANDAGA RIVER UPSTREAM TO ELM LAKE

The best access for a trip up the Kunjamuk to Elm Lake is by the parking area 0.5 mile south on NY 8/30 of the main intersection in the village of Speculator. From here it is easy to launch a canoe into the Sacandaga River and paddle 1.8 miles downstream to the mouth of the Kunjamuk. It is also possible to launch a canoe from the parking area on NY 30, 2 miles east of the village. The shore is swampy, but the spot is almost opposite, due south, of the confluence of the rivers.

Starting at the village parking area, you canoe in a long arc to the east to intersect the Kunjamuk, which flows in from the north. The rivers meet in a huge marsh immediately west of Rift Hill, the only dominant feature in that part of the flood plain.

Turn north and follow the slow meanders of the Kunjamuk; its loops and squiggles appear to have been etched in the sand by a giant with very bad script. You reach the new hiker's bridge for the trail to Kunjamuk Cave in 3.5 miles but the turnings of the Kunjamuk add at least 1.5 miles to the distance you travel. Allow two hours to paddle this far. If you wish a side trip, the short walking excursion to the Kunjamuk Cave (section 33) takes about thirty minutes.

Another hour of paddling north will put you in Elm Lake. Very few portages are encountered along this section of the Kunjamuk. Of course, new beaver work may change all that, but it is for the moment an easy trip. The best time to canoe here is in moderately low water; then there is little current to fight. The river is passable even in low water. Some of the time the river flows between marshy shores, but sand flats are often visible. The entire valley was at one time a glacial lake, collecting deep sand deposits through which the river recut its sinuous path. Near the exposed sand flats north of the cave there are lovely views north to Dug, East, and Upper Pine mountains.

ELM LAKE NORTH TO LONG LEVEL BRIDGE

The 2-mile direct distance between Elm Lake and the Long Level Bridge is more than doubled by the river's meanderings. Over the first 0.5 mile the river appears lost in the marshes, and in places alders grow across almost its full width. Closer to the bridge the number decreases only somewhat. Allow two hours for a one-way canoe trip in this section.

Birding here, as in the north, is fantastic. One July day, I counted six kinds of warblers, the olive-sided flycatcher, and a multitude of hummingbirds along the river.

If you have a friend with a suitable four-wheel-drive vehicle who can drop you and your canoe off at the Long Level Bridge, you will find that the trip south through Elm Lake to Speculator is a good outing. The whole round trip from Speculator to the Iron Bridge and return is a very strenuous day's workout. You may find the round trip to Elm Lake is all you can manage in one day.

UPPER KUNJAMUK—THE LONG LEVEL BRIDGE NORTH TO THE FISH BARRIER DAM

Between the Upper Bridge (now closed to vehicles), which is 1 mile south of the Fish Barrier Dam, and the Long Level Bridge above Elm Lake, the Kunjamuk remains fairly clear of deadfalls. Low water can still make this run difficult, but it is a section to be savored. The raspberries are as good as ever and you can enjoy the views of Upper Pine Mountain's cliffs without undue struggling.

The birding here is good throughout the summer months. Flocks of cedar waxwings and ducks can be found along the quiet waters. Elderberry, Fall Clematis, the sweet-smelling Bedstraw, Swamp Milkweed, Joe-Pye weed, and cherry trees overhang the river bed. The fallen trees and huge bare elm stumps that dot the swamps are beautiful in a grotesque way. The hemlock roots that contribute to the current obstacles will only weather into more sculpturally intricate forms. The strangest part of the scenery is the riverbed; it is carved in sand containing almost no rocks. The only rocks or pebbles in the upper Kunjamuk appear south near the Iron Bridge.

Between the Upper Bridge and the Fish Barrier Dam, a distance of less than 1 mile, there are several obstacles, among them beaver dams, which help raise the water level; alder patches growing nearly across the river; and some stretches so shallow in low water that canoeing is impossible. Portaging may be sufficiently difficult that you may want to omit this stretch or portage via the road if you are trying to reach state land to camp.

To arrange a drop-off at the Upper Bridge, use Fly Creek Road to the Long Level Bridge, about 0.7 mile north of the bridge over Silver Brook and continue north on East Road. You can still drive to the Upper Bridge, even if vehicles cannot cross on it, and you can launch your canoe beside the bridge.

ABOVE THE FISH BARRIER DAM

The best canoeing on the upper Kunjamuk is above the Fish Barrier Dam, a small wood and stone structure built to prevent pickerel and other warm-water species from reaching the trout waters upstream. Unfortunately, the dam did not keep out the undesired species and the UMP states that the dam will not be replaced when it deteriorates, so enjoy this section while it lasts. To reach this access, take East Road (section 32) to the intersection 0.2 mile from its end and turn right (east). In 0.4 mile, you come to a parking place at the edge of state land. There is a chain across the end of the road that vehicles have gone around to drive the last 200 yards to the dam, which is neither necessary nor legal. It is an easy canoe carry if you park at the designated spot and portage to the dam.

The chain at the end of the road is a threshold to a different world. The timbered lands along International Paper Company's stretch of the Kunjamuk are lovely, but the state land is infinitely more beautiful. Huge hemlock and pine grow in the sand flats, with mosses and ferns beneath instead of brambles and berries.

There is a very handsome camping spot beside the water near the dam, under a giant pine tree. Cardinal flowers grace the small swamp below the dam.

Upper Kunjamuk, above the Fish Barrier Dam

The canoeable section north of the Fish Barrier Dam is scarcely 1.5 miles long. Weird patterns of the skeletons of alders indicate the recent flooding of the impounded water, which is unusually rich in plant life and food. In the midst of this cemetery of stumps and trees are four huge beaver houses and over two dozen muskrat houses.

The floating plant with leaves like the lotus that braces these waters in late July is called the watershield, *Brasenia schreberi*. The underside of the leaves have a thick coating of a jelly-like substance and the flowers are small with tiny purple petals and sepals.

The quiet, swampy waters are home to many birds. Great blue heron nest here, but the few pairs of eastern kingbirds, with their white-banded tails and distinctive flight, are even more spectacular. The kingbirds seem to hover vertically, as if suspended by their wing tips, darting to catch insects and returning to their favorite stump a few feet above the water. Tamarack and hemlock serve as perches for flocks of cedar waxwings.

The view south from the river is framed by Upper Pine Mountain on the east and Dug and East mountains on the west. The cliffs on Upper Pine Mountain are sharply defined. A canoe and camping trip to this point would be delightful. With a four-wheel-drive vehicle to drop a canoe close to the edge of state land, this is an easy half-day paddle.

37 Rock Pond from the South

Trail, old road, campsite, fishing, swimming, cross-country skiing
2.5 miles, 1¼ hours, relatively level

Rock Pond has all the ingredients for a perfect camping destination: a high, evergreen-covered bank overlooking the clear water of a distant, secluded pond. However, the trailhead for the good short path to the pond is reached by a long, difficult drive over International Paper Company lands. Alternate routes from the north, which do not cross International Paper Company land, are described in section 56 and 65.

The difficulties of approaching Rock Pond and Long Pond have not isolated them. In fact, because they are remote wilderness destinations, they are very popular with fishermen and a number of campers.

Access is from a parking turnout in the midst of a forest of notable pines

on the edge of state land, at the end of an 8-mile, hour-long, jostling drive on East Road, north from Speculator. The transition from International Paper Company land to deep forest is even more dramatic along this road than it is on the way to the Fish Barrier Dam (section 36). On a warm day, the hot, dry, sandy smells of the lower Kunjamuk will give way to the cool, damp, moss and evergreen smells of the wilderness over a distance of less than a hundred feet. You feel as if you have crossed an invisible barrier, walking from the world of man to the world of nature.

The route commences by immediately crossing Cisco Brook on a nearly decayed bridge. The footpath, which is not marked, follows an old logging road for the entire distance to Rock Pond. After a twenty-minute walk, there are views to the east across the Kunjamuk. The path continues through a plantation of large pine with a thick, low, heavily browsed understory.

A mile north, within a half hour, the path forks in the midst of the reforestation area. The state lean-to that used to be near the fork—it is still marked on the USGS maps—has long since disappeared. If you take a thirty-minute round-trip excursion down the right fork you'll walk through a red pine plantation to the site of the old bridge over the Kunjamuk. One glance at the flooded lands will convince you that special reconnaissance is necessary before walking the entire Kunjamuk Road described in section 65. However, as that section details, this route has become very popular for ski-touring.

All of the road and path so far would be good for ski-touring; the only problem is that access from the south in winter is only by snowmobile or by an already *very long* ski trek.

Return to the junction and continue on the west fork toward Rock Pond. The trail arcs to the west, away from the Kunjamuk, through mixed hardwood forests where a few large popple and huge birch are scattered among the maple. The route becomes covered with mixed evergreens as it approaches Rock Pond.

The sparsely marked trail has good foot tread and is very easy to follow. It wanders on top of sinuous humps, which elevate the old roadbed less than a dozen feet above the surrounding land, but just enough to make the roadway good and dry. Spruce and hemlock are the characteristic cover on the sandy soil of the eskers.

The trail dips to the outlet of Rock Pond where a path veers to the left, west, up through a small gorge by the pond's outlet. It leads to the pond in 200 yards. A lovely campsite surrounded by pine, hemlock, and spruce is north of the outlet, and beyond it a steep ledge provides a lovely vista across the pond to tiny spruce-covered islands and promontories.

The water of Rock Pond is clear, the bottom is rocky, and the swimming is good. The lake has been stocked with brook trout.

38 Long Pond from the South
Trail, hiking, camping, fishing
3.5 miles, under 2 hours, relatively level

Long Pond lies just northeast of Rock Pond, sharing the latter's trailhead and reputation as a great camping destination. However, many people think Long Pond has superior fishing and more handsome surroundings. A backdrop of long, parallel rock formations borders its shores. These echo the line of the long northeast trending fault that created the pond.

To reach Long Pond, continue north past Rock Pond at 2.5 miles on the trail along the roadway from the International Paper Company's Kunjamuk Tract (section 37). The distance between the ponds is about 1 mile and will take no more than twenty minutes to walk. Although this is an official trail, it is currently unmarked; nevertheless, it is well used and easy to follow.

When you reach Long Pond look for the informal path that traverses the entire western shore, connecting many camping sites beneath the hemlock-covered ridge west of the pond. You may find a few of the sites littered with garbage, although the interior ranger cleans them regularly. You can usually find boats on the pond, though they lack paddles. You may wish to bring along a paddle or even an inflatable boat. Fishermen regularly visit Long Pond in search of the brook trout that are stocked here.

The eastern shore of the pond is lined with a small rock-faced hill from whose summit (section 39) there are exceptionally fine views. Kunjamuk Mountain and its cliffs are visible north of the pond.

The best camping spot on the western shore is at the rocky tip of the peninsula that thrusts north into the upper part of the pond. One of the informal paths along the west shore leads to it. There are leeches in the pond, so avoid swimming where the shoreline is muddy. The deep pool to the west of the rocky promontory offers the best swimming of all.

As an interior wilderness camping destination, this pond rates with Siamese Ponds both for beauty and use. Interconnecting routes from the north are detailed in sections 55 and 56 and a bushwhack from the east is mentioned in section 65.

View south along the Kunjamuk Valley from Long Pond Cliffs

39   Cliffs above Long Pond

Easy bushwhack, good views

No matter which way you choose to climb to the cliffs on the hill east of Long Pond, the views are worth the effort. The cliff top is bare for many feet behind the edge and the rock slopes back, away from the cliff edge, so it is possible to find a safe viewing perch. From the southern end of the cliff top you can see beyond the Kunjamuk Valley to a part of Humphrey Mountain, with the Big Range spreading south of it. Also in the south you can pick up the distinctive sharp nose of Upper Pine Mountain, and to its west Dug and East mountains. Long Pond Ridge obstructs a part of the view to the west, but north of the ridge you will see the tops of Snowy and Squaw mountains, which rise on the far side of Indian Lake. At the head of the pond is the cliff-covered face of Kunjamuk Mountain. South of west on the distant horizon you should see Page and Blue Ridge mountains. Also to the south, immediately below the cliff, is a dark gem of a little unnamed pond. And, of course, this is obviously the best spot from which to see Long Pond.

The trail from Rock Pond to Long Pond (section 38) takes you to the southern end of Long Pond. You could begin a bushwhack to the cliffs here, walking east around the southern end of the pond, and then swinging north to climb the hill behind the cliffs. However, beavers have flooded several streams and created a huge marshy area south and east of the pond. As a result, I recommend that you start your climb to the cliffs by bushwhacking around the north end of the pond to the northeast corner and heading east to the lower cliffs. Search about for a safe route up them, then turn south and continue climbing along the ridgeline to the exposed cliff tops. Unfortunately, dense evergreen thickets still make walking difficult.

Actually, the preferred approach involves a bit of luck. If there is a safe boat on the pond, paddle across to the southeastern shore, immediately south of the cliffs. From here climb north along the ridge. For navigation, this bushwhack route rates easy; for travel, walking is rough at best. Climbing by the easiest way may still take nearly an hour from the pond's shore.

If you are camping at Long Pond you will have ample time to include the bushwhack to the cliffs as part of your stay. If you want to climb the cliffs on a one-day outing, remember you will need nearly two hours for the round-trip drive to the trailhead from NY 8/30, almost four hours for the round-trip walk from the trailhead to Long Pond via the trail, and a minimum of two hours for the round-trip bushwhack to the cliffs from the pond, using the shortest route across the lake by boat, so allow plenty of time. A longer, but ultimately no more difficult, alternate is suggested in section 65.

40 Dug Mountain Silver Mine

Logging road

It is only a short walk to the Dug Mountain Silver Mine if you have the four-wheel-drive transportation necessary to travel on the roads that lead to it through International Paper Company's Kunjamuk Tract. A dirt road parallels Silver Brook, heading west, and then southwest, from the logging road on the west side of the Kunjamuk (see section 32). The Silver Brook Road is sometimes passable by four-wheel-drive vehicles.

The mine is near the head of the Silver Brook valley in the saddle between Dug and East mountains, not far beyond the last cabin on the road. The road is now marked as a snowmobile trail, and the trail continues southwest through Whiskey Brook valley and the bog and marshes surrounding it and back to East Road.

Oldtimers report the mine had a shaft dug 85 feet deep into the mountain, but recent visitors report finding only a depression in the ground. Claims that silver was actually mined here have been disputed. In fact, there is little evidence that this and several other mines in Hamilton County were anything but schemes to make money for the speculators who filed a series of mining claims and incorporated a handful of gold and silver mining companies in the early 1880s. A sharp-eyed explorer might find the shaft, but there is no chance of discovering ore.

You can reach the mine in an easy walk of just over 1 mile along the dirt road beside Silver Brook. The walk can be continued southwest on the snowmobile trail around East Mountain and then back to intersect East Road. In summer this route is rarely used except by a few fishermen who try their luck along Whiskey Brook.

41   Robbs Creek Road
Birding, walking, skiing, hunting

With an IP permit, you can enjoy the best of birding along the Robbs Creek Road. It is a nice walk for those who want the level base of a dirt road; it is currently possible to drive the road without a four-wheel-drive vehicle, but it may not always be so.

Drive south 1.8 miles along Old Route 30 from its northern intersection with NY 30 and turn left, north, onto the Robbs Creek Road. You certainly want to leave the road at the bridge over Robbs Creek, 1.1 miles up the road. A path of sorts leads from a turnout on the north side of the bridge about a hundred yards to Robbs Creek, where there is a charming small waterfall. Just downstream is the confluence with Hayes Creek.

Driving north, in 0.1 mile you pass the Hayes Creek Road, a right fork. Beyond there are marshes, and you might spot a marsh harrier, cedar waxwing, or redstart. At 3.1 miles there is a new beaver dam east of the road on a small stream, which may erode the track you are following. The beaver flow is home to nesting black ducks. At 3.25 miles, a left fork leads to a bridge over Robbs Creek. Here you should definitely be walking, since the bridge is deteriorating, but you can follow the dirt road until it forks and gradually loses itself in a maze of logging tracks.

At 4.2 miles, the end of the road, a bridge over the creek, left fork, is out. The roadway continues (not for driving) and gradually disappears after it crosses onto state land.

42 Hayes Flow
Hiking, fishing, hunting

This unofficial path on state land is remarkably easy to follow. It leads from the Robbs Creek Road, 3 miles east to the flow, for a relatively easy and very delightful walk to a really remote flow, one reached only occasionally by hunters and fishermen.

Park adjacent to the Robbs Creek Road, 1.2 miles from its start, and walk along the roadway to the east for three or four minutes. Notice that you are following Hayes Creek. As the roadway turns left and uphill, another old road forks right to continue along the creek. Only the intersection is concealed in brush. In just over a quarter mile you cross onto state land. At about 1 mile, a brisk twenty-five-minute walk, the roadway leads to a rock crossing of Hayes Creek.

A couple of minutes beyond, no more than 200 yards, the path forks. The right leads uphill and along a long level before descending to join the left fork, which stays right at creekside. You may want to follow the right fork in wet weather, for the other can be very muddy. However, be warned that it does almost disappear in blowdowns at several points. It will take about forty minutes, part of it spent looking for the overgrown path, to reach the eastern intersection with the creek path.

The half-mile route along the rocky creek is very pretty and it takes no more than fifteen minutes to the point where the path swings uphill away from a swampy area. In ten minutes of winding uphill, you reach the intersection and in ten more minutes you reach a small clearing which hunters have used for a fall season camp. A path from the northeastern corner of the campsite leads downhill to the creek again. A path from the eastern side leads in fifteen minutes to a beaver dam at the outlet of the flow.

There do not seem to be any paths around the flow, which has pretty wet shores. However, you can find a picnic spot from which to observe the spruce-capped peninsula which is about midway north along the flow. Buckhorn Mountain looms to the southeast of the flow with the pass between it and Macomber just east of south, and Macomber itself a little west of south.

43 The Big Range

Hiking, birding, hunting

A large rectangle of IP's land was purchased by the state in 1985. This added the summits of the Big Range and the upper reaches of Shingle Brook to the Siamese Ponds Wilderness. In spite of the fact that logging roads cross the tract and in spite of its past logging history, this is wild country. The road system will make good hiking access for some years to come.

When Colvin first surveyed the Adirondacks, he wrote of a bear chase south and east from Indian Lake. In all likelihood it ended in the Big Range, which is still notable for its wildlife as well as its birds.

Access is easiest from Fly Creek Road, following it 3.5 miles to the fork to Long Level Bridge. Stop at the bridge where you can see Dug Mountain on the left, west, and Cross and Pine Point mountains to the right, with Big Range filling the northeastern horizon.

If you continue north on Fly Creek Road for 0.4 mile, you cross Pine Point Brook, and 0.1 mile beyond, the road forks left. Go straight ahead on an increasingly rough road that minimally requires a high wheelbase. At 1.2 miles you overlook wetlands on the left. There is an endless chain of beaver dams, "hydro projects," on the little stream. At just short of 2 miles you see the first of the Upper Pine Lakes. The road is almost impassible beyond this point. At 2.4 miles, you cross a bridge over Shingle Brook, near the border of state land. You have to park south of the bridge; and it may be, depending on the road's condition, that you will have to walk part or all of the 2.4 miles from Long Level to this bridge.

Continue walking along the road past the bridge. Immediately you pass two roads which fork right, steeply uphill. Stay left and in about twenty minutes you pass a fork to the left. At thirty-five minutes, after a long, gently uphill walk, you stay right as the road begins to swing from a northwesterly to a southeasterly direction. After about a fifty-five-minute walk you will find yourself in a large meadow with a big beaver pond. Across it to the southeast you can see the Big Range covered with dying red spruce.

Two logging roads, each with numerous skid trails, head up the Big Range from the southeast corner of the meadow. One, heading southeast, leads to a high valley with views northwest toward Snowy Mountain. The route south is very steep and overgrown and does not lead all the way to the summit of the Big Range, but adventurous bushwhackers will want to push all the way to the summit ridge where openings offer magnificent views to the north and east. Depending on the amount of time you wish to spend bushwhacking on the hill, you should allow a minimum of four hours for exploring, at least another hour for the southern climb.

44 Shingle Brook Valley
Hiking, birding, hunting

This trek starts along either of the two right forks that are immediately north of the bridge over Shingle Brook (section 43). The roads join about 0.3 mile uphill and parallel Shingle Brook in an arc to the southeast. Near their junction, you can hear a small waterfall on the brook. You will want to leave the road to explore its handsome ledges. Because this section has been acquired by the state, you should expect the continuing route to become less distinct and gradually wilder. Already, beaver activity has changed some of the traditional roads in the area.

After the roads join, the route continues the arc, then heads due south, ending after a forty-minute walk at a wonderful beaver meadow. Upstream, there is a second flooded area, behind a more recent beaver dam, but downstream, all that remains is a series of washed-out dams and meadows where there once was a huge flow. From the far side, the west, there are lovely views of the northwest face of the Big Range across the almost eerily desolate remains of the flow.

The principal road once followed the western side and you can follow it back (though it is rapidly becoming overgrown) to the foot of the flow where a natural rock dam once provided a ford across the stream. This point is but 100 yards from the logging road you followed south, but the intersection is already so concealed in new growth that it is impossible to describe how to find it from the north. But walking around the flow in a clockwise direction is all that you need to explore this upland valley.

From Speculator to Indian Lake

MUCH OF THE land on both sides of NY 30, from Speculator north to within two miles of Mason Lake and Panther Pond, is owned by International Paper Company. All the permit descriptions in section 30 apply to these lands, which offer several good adventures, covered in sections 45 through 47. Section 46 is perfect for bird watching.

45 Whiskey Brook
Waterfall, picnic site, logging road, cross-country skiing

Almost 2.5 miles north of Speculator on NY 30, there is a parking turnout on the east side of the road beside a small stream. A hundred feet from the road, but completely concealed in summer, Whiskey Brook tumbles from the east over a small, but exquisite falls. Beer cans in the midst of the jumble of rocks will remind you that you are not at a pristine location, but it is not a bad spot for a picnic for those who do not walk any distances. A small stone fireplace is located on the south side of the falls in a remarkable quiet and secluded, tiny, spruce-shaded clearing.

One-half mile beyond the picnic area turnout, a log road leads through International Paper Company land from NY 30 east to the bogs and marshes along the north side of Whiskey Brook. A snowmobile trail is routed along this road and traverses the frozen marshes in winter. In summer the bogs and marshes are difficult to reach, but the roads to them are available for hikers with permits.

46 Whitaker Lake Road
Jeep road, walking route

The jeep road to Whitaker Lake, 5.5 miles north of Speculator on NY 30, is marked by a huge boulder whose resemblance to a pig's snout has been emphasized by yearly doses of fresh paint—graffiti that not all find humorous. The jeep road is suitable for ordinary vehicles for only a half mile, as far as the fork to Camp Deerfoot, a boys' camp on Whitaker Lake. The road leads through IP land, for which a permit is required, to a private inholding on Dug Mountain Ponds. Further access is barred 2.5 miles from NY 30, opposite a charming string of ponds that are excellent birding spots. The recent extension of the private inholding to include an exclusive leasehold from IP encompasses the north flanks of Dug Mountain, including the summit area with its views described in the earlier edition of this guide. That bushwhack, therefore, is omitted from this guide.

For those who prefer walking open roads to obscure wooded trails, the 2 miles beyond the fork to Camp Deerfoot are ideal. Open woods have the advantages of birds, butterflies, and berries, and this one is well endowed with all three. Blackberries are lush in mid-summer and butterflies seem to give the wild field-flowers lining the road a second set of blossoms.

There is a slight rise around a small hill west of the ponds, but otherwise the road is fairly level, making the 4-mile round trip an easy two-hour walk, unless you pause to bird.

47 Indian Clearing and Dug Mountain Falls
Easy bushwhack, old roads, waterfall, picnic site

The triangle between Dug Mountain Brook, the Jessup River, and Whitaker Lake is crisscrossed with old logging roads and paths so overgrown in places that following them must be considered bushwhacking. The "hub" of this area is a place called Indian Clearing.

Research has so far failed to explain the clearing's name. There was certainly a clearing, but whether it was used by Indians or resulted from logging and farming activity is unknown. Parts of the main old road through the clearing are very overgrown.

To reach Indian Clearing, take the Whitaker Lake Road (section 46) east from NY 30 for 1.5 miles. Here an abandoned road heads north from the rutted and rock-strewn jeep road. Park near the turn and walk north along the abandoned road. In five minutes you will reach state land.

In 0.2 mile you come to a road barrier; just beyond it the bridge over Cannon Brook has almost collapsed. After walking a total of a half hour,

Upper Falls on Dug Mountain Brook

you should reach another fork, this one in a small field where saplings and dense brush grow over your head, almost concealing the junction. This is part of Indian Clearing.

Your route is the more obvious one, west. Within five minutes, the road curves to the north, and a second old road forks left, west, this one so overgrown you may not notice it. The continuing route has been walked and occasionally flagged and you should be able to follow it as it curves west again. Watch here, for the outlet of Dug Mountain Ponds is less than 100 yards north of the old road.

If you leave the route here and walk to the stream, you can follow it west for about five minutes, as it begins to plunge through a small draw. Here, you will find a lovely 30-foot waterfall. Most of the year, you can hop rocks across the brook below the waterfall and pick up a faint path on the north shore, following it west to the Jessup River, which is here broadening into one of the long fingers of Indian Lake.

A picnic spot, also reached by canoe from Indian Lake, marks the confluence where the smaller stream tumbles over a square-jointed ledge that creates the lower falls on the brook. In summer, the water is usually low enough so you can hop rocks across the brook here as well, and continue a loop to the old road. A path heads uphill, southeast from the lower falls, to intersect the road. It is faint, but marked with a few blazes. A left turn takes you back to Indian Clearing and Whitaker Lake Road. Note: you could have made the loop in the reverse direction, but the place where the faint path leaves the road is hard to find.

Figure forty-five minutes for the 1.5-mile return, an hour or more for the segment past the falls. The whole loop with bushwhack or path route to the upper falls is only 3.5 miles. If you want to follow other old roads in the area, you will find there is a faint path along the Jessup.

48   Jessup River
Canoeing, campsite, fishing

The best canoeing on the Jessup River is west of NY 30, outside the area described in this guide. You will find the section east of NY 30 just as handsome, but all too short. The river traverses a meandering course in flowed lands between the highway and rapids that usually prevent canoeists from continuing into Indian Lake. Early in the season, when Indian Lake is full, the rapids almost disappear, but in low water, or when Indian

Lake has been drawn down, the length of the stretch of rapids increases. Sometimes water is so low that the area of the rapids seems paved in rocks.

Almost 7 miles north of Speculator, NY 30 bridges the Jessup River. North of the bridge, on the west side of the road, there is space to park. A path on the northeast side of the bridge leads to a clearing and a well-used campsite. The southeast side of the bridge offers the easiest canoe launching, which fishermen routinely use, as the Jessup has been heavily stocked with land-locked salmon.

There is a shoal beneath the bridge, but when you head downstream, you will find the river is deep and easily navigable except for a random submerged log. It is only a thirty-minute paddle through the flat water to the edge of the Jessup's rapids.

In high water, when the rapids are nearly flooded, boats sometimes continue downstream to Indian Lake. That this is not easy or generally advisable is indicated by the numerous scrape marks and aluminum skids on the rocks in the stream bed.

If you want to continue to the Dug Mountain Falls and the picnic site on Indian Lake, follow the path which begins at the head of the rapids on the east side of the Jessup.

49 Panther Pond
Short path, easy bushwhack

Panther Pond is a small, boggy pond east of Mason Lake. It is a lovely destination for a very short walk and is an excellent place to search for pitcher plants and blueberries and to watch for birds.

Park at the turnout on the west side of NY 30 at Mason Lake. Walk south along the east side of the highway for 800 feet until you see a single round wood post over five feet high. It has a yellow painted circle near the top. This marks the start of an abandoned snowmobile trail that heads towards Dug Mountain Falls and the Jessup River. The trail is generally easy to walk and corduroy has been placed in the few swampy areas. There are occasional snowmobile trail markers, blazes on trees, and yellow circles painted on trees. It is possible to lose the trail, however, when you detour around several blowdowns, because witch hobble and maple obscure the route.

After you have been on the faint trail for eight to ten minutes you should catch a glimpse of Panther Pond in the small valley to the left. A number of indistinct paths head down the ridge toward it. The north and west shores have the best bogs. The easiest approach to the sphagnum mats that form the pond's shoreline is down high ground to the south shore along the first visible path. The best place to view bog plants is around on the north shore.

To return to the trail, head south back up the ridge. The snowmobile trail is faint, but if you look carefully for it, remembering it is about 80 feet in elevation above the pond, you should intersect it with no trouble.

50 Jessup River/West Side
Path, picnic site

The abandoned snowmobile trail, whose beginning is described in section 49, continues generally east to the Jessup River, ending at a picnic site opposite the Dug Mountain Falls. No camping is allowed. A second picnic site is directly opposite, beside the falls. Hikers will find it difficult to cross the Jessup to the Dug Mountain Falls side. In very low water, the river can be forded a short ways upstream. However, although wading is not difficult, it will be a wet crossing; there are just not enough stones to make dry rock-hopping possible, even in low water.

As indicated in section 49, there are occasional snowmobile markers, blazes, and yellow paint and the route is generally easy to follow with a good foot tread. There are a number of blowdowns and it is sometimes difficult to locate the trail again after detouring around them. Be sure to search and find it before going on.

After about fifteen minutes' walk from NY 30 there is a trail to the right marked with some red tape. Take the left fork, which has a snowmobile trail marker.

The trail passes through an open forest of mature hardwoods with maples and yellow birch over one hundred feet tall. It is an attractive, easy walk. Bring your bathing suit along as the picnic site is at the point where Indian Lake begins and swimming is excellent. The shoreline falls off rapidly so it is not appropriate for small children.

The 1.2-mile one-way walk can be done in forty minutes.

Indian Lake

WHEN SETTLERS FIRST visited the valley of the Indian River, they saw a wild river connecting a series of three small lakes. Steep mountains ranged west of the river, defining the long fault valley through which it flowed. Magnificent forests of pine and spruce filled the valley and grew up the slopes of the mountains. These attracted the first settlers, lumbermen, who dammed the river in the 1840s to form one long lake on which they could easily float logs to their mills.

A second, higher dam was built in 1861, by which time Indian Lake village at the lake's northern end had grown to a community of 300. The high dam that creates the present fourteen-mile-long lake was built in 1898.

The transition to the present beautiful lake was not easy; a fisherman writing in 1853 described the trip down the newly created lake as "monotonous and uninteresting. Much of the timber is dead and from a dam constructed at the foot of Indian Lake, which backs up the water for many miles. What a place for a man to select and bring up a family in. I wish he had kept away, for the stumps and log buildings were an eyesore and a detraction from what otherwise would have been magnificent scenery. Still the wild rugged mountains are all around and many a peak may be seen fading blue in the distance."

Today, you will see a handsome lake stretching with long, thin fingers along the fault lines between the range of mountains. Only when the water level has been lowered, an event that occurs regularly in late summer or early fall, will you see the weathered remains of stumps along the shoreline, to remind you of the lake's origin.

51 Indian Lake Campsites
Canoeing, camping

There are many isolated campsites ranged along the remote eastern shore of Indian Lake, and others on the many islands that dot it. All are accessible only by boat. Because they are dispersed, well-designed, and well-maintained, a credit to the New York State Department of Environmental Conservation, they provide a wild and primitive camping experience.

Access to the sixty state-run Indian Lake Island campsites and permits to use them are available at the Island Caretaker Headquarters just north of Lewey Lake Campsite on NY 30. A boat-launching site that can handle anything from canoes to larger motor boats is adjacent to the headquarters. The caretaker will provide you with an excellent map of Indian Lake and the campsites and some good advice on lake camping. He will also collect the fee for use of the campsites and picnic areas.

Each site has a fireplace, a privy, and a table and bench. Some are also equipped with tent platforms. Although the settings vary, each has a special view of the lake, its islands, and the dominant range of mountains to its west.

There are times and conditions when reaching the campsites by canoe can be all but impossible. Southwest winds can churn the lake into waves that are dangerous for small boats, so plan your outings here accordingly. Besides swimming, sunning, and canoeing, these campsites offer access to the walks described in sections 55 through 58.

Indian Lake is manmade and summer water levels vary. Low water can change the approach to some picnic areas and campsites.

52   Indian Lake Picnic Sites
Picnicking, swimming

Four areas around Indian Lake have been set aside by the state for day use only. In addition to picnicking and swimming, each has something special to offer. Please note that no camping and no animals are allowed at these sites.

Dug Mountain Brook Picnic Areas. The easiest way to reach the Dug Mountain Brook picnic sites is by boat from the state launching site by the Indian Island Caretaker Headquarters off NY 30, although hikers can reach it from Indian Clearing (section 47). Dug Mountain Brook empties into the Jessup River just upstream of its mouth on one of the two long fingers of Indian Lake; the one-way distance of 8 miles makes the trip fairly long for canoeing. The channels are deep and power boats regularly visit the area.

There are four picnic tables and a fireplace. The end of the no-camping area is a ten-minute walk across Dug Mountain Brook and south along the path beside the Jessup, and people do camp there.

The falls on Dug Mountain beside the picnic area make this especially attractive. It is well-shaded for hot days and has a good sandy beach extending into the Jessup River for swimming. The beach slopes gradually (it is only four feet deep twenty-five feet from shore), so it is perfect for young children.

Moose Island Picnic Area. Located on the northern end of Moose Island about midway along Indian Lake, this picnic area is on a point surrounded on three sides with a sandy beach. A good deep water approach exists on the western shore. If you approach the island from the north or northeast, be careful because of the rock shoals that may be just beneath the water's surface, depending on the water level.

There are three picnic tables and a fireplace on the point, and a second fireplace and a single table in a more secluded spot about 50 feet from the main area. The tables are shaded by maples, beech, and balsam, and the island behind the site is heavily wooded.

Parsons Point Picnic Area. The only day-use picnic area on the western shore of Indian Lake is on a rugged and rocky bluff. From the water, you might not suspect its existence, except for the signs nailed on trees by the shore.

As you approach the rocky shoreline, however, you will see two picnic tables and a fireplace. Fifty feet to the right and on a hill back in the trees is another fireplace and table. This site is so secluded that you can scarcely see the lake from it. The bathing area is partly rock and partly sand. A much better place for children is just north of Campsite #12 on the north side of Parsons Point, 100 yards away.

Normans Cove. Indian Lake's northernmost picnic site is on a peninsula north of Normans Cove, which in turn is north of the northernmost large island, Kirpens.

Three picnic tables are clustered around the only fireplace in the area, and a fourth table stands on a tree-shaded knoll at the cove's entrance.

The cove effectively protects the bathing area and boat landing from the north and west winds. At the eastern shore of the cove a flat rock with a faint white circle painted on it marks the beginning of the trail to the summit of Baldface Mountain (section 58), which has a superb view of the lake and the surrounding mountains.

53   Indian Lake Campsites Sampler
Camping

The Indian Lake campsites are identified by number, the count beginning at the lake's northern end. While each is special, a few deserve extra notice and cautions. Some sites can handle several tents, while others can accommodate only a single small one. Check with the ranger at the headquarters building off NY 30 (see introduction to this chapter).

#1. The northernmost campsite lies above a small cliff on the eastern shore of the lake. Just to its north is a small sandy beach and landing.

#3. The Kirpens Island site is sheltered in very deep woods, perfect for a hot summer day. The steep-slanted rock landing poses a problem for unloading boats and does not offer good swimming for young children.

#5. Campsite #5 is located in a well-manicured stand of spruce on the east shore right at the edge of the water, where there is usually a breeze to keep the bugs away. It is a choice location for enjoying sunsets.

#12. Even though this site is on the west shore of the lake, where the highway runs, it can only be reached by water. Watch your approach, as there are numerous rocks below the lake's surface about 50 feet from shore. A very large sand beach about 100 feet long, just north of the site, makes it perfect for swimming.

#21. This site on the western shore of Sand Island is tucked in a grove of paper birch and has a moderate deep-water approach.

#27. This campsite, at John Mack Landing, has one of the best shore-lines, with a great sandy beach.

#28. Located in John Mack Bay, this site receives little sunlight because it is sheltered by a stand of large beech trees and lies in the shadow of Gates Hill on the opposite side of the bay. The trail to John Mack Pond (section 54) leaves the bay just east of the campsite.

#49. Located north of a small wooded knoll called the Chocolate Bar, Campsite #49 is by the mouth of McGinn Brook, which empties into the Jessup River section of Indian Lake. A small shallow pool in the brook and smooth rock slabs make this a delightful campsite for families with small children who like to sail little boats.

54 Watch Hill

Path, short and steep climb, great views

An unmarked dirt road forks right, east, from NY 30 1.2 miles south of the parking area for Snowy Mountain, 3.9 miles north of the entrance for the Indian Lake Islands Campground. There is room to park off the highway near the dirt road, which will lead you to a surprisingly good adventure.

Follow the dirt road as it heads west, crosses Griffin Brook on a deteriorating bridge, and curves north, paralleling the highway for just over ten minutes to a sign that reads "Pinnacle—Watch Hill." Turn right along the indicated narrow path that is occasionally marked with red squares. In 200 yards, a path forks left—this is an alternate, longer, and gentler climb used by horseback riders from Timberlock, the lodge a mile south of the beginning of this hike.

The path that is straight ahead climbs sharply up the hill, then curves south along its ridgeline. The longer route joins from the north, and the path, now quite narrow, mounts a couple of rock outcrops in a beautiful, deep hemlock forest. The path then winds south, dipping into a saddle, then up another crest to the top of a cliff, overlooking the deep valley to the west and mountains beyond.

The third view spot is the best, for it looks south along Indian Lake from a perch precipitously placed above a cliff. This point is almost forty minutes from the highway; the return is faster.

Another path continues to lakeshore but does not make a loop with this red trail. If you poke about to the northwest of the outcrop, you will find a faint path, occasionally marked with yellow squares, that heads steeply down toward the lake. But, after the first steep drop, the path turns westerly and parallels the shore of Indian Lake, well above lake level. The path descends gently and is tantalizingly slow about approaching the lake. When it does, it emerges beside an old fireplace to a lovely sandy shore in a bay. Mark the place well because it is impossible to distinguish it from other points along the several curved beaches.

Both of these paths are marked by people from Timberlock. The red portion is easy to follow. The yellow portion is pretty well marked for the descent, but there are few squares marking the ascending route and at least three places where you have to search about for the continuing route, especially where it winds across the heads of several draws.

If you want to find the Watch Hill path from the water, walk along the beaches about 0.5 mile north of the buildings at Timberlock and look into

the woods for the fireplace. The descent from the Pinnacle is about thirty minutes; it is a bit longer to climb back up.

55   John Mack Pond

Trail, camping, hiking, fishing
1.7 miles, 1 hour plus canoe trip, 195-foot climb

Place names can be so frustrating. Sometimes a family name is a real clue to an area's settlers, but often no trace of the people so-named can be found. This is the case for John Mack Pond. According to Ted Aber, Hamilton County historian, there is no mention of John Mack in local records. All that survives is the doubtful tale that the pond was named for a John McKenzie who came from Canada after getting an Indian girl in trouble. Although we may never know for whom it was named or why, John Mack Pond deserves a visit.

The trailhead is accessible only by water. Park in the designated area at the Indian Lake Islands Campground Headquarters, opposite Lewey Lake. Pay the day-use fee and obtain a map of the lake and its campsites from the ranger. It takes about one hour and fifteen minutes to paddle by canoe northeast on Indian Lake, unless you are paddling into the wind. During the trip, looking up the lake, there are tremendous views of the high peaks in the distance. Paddle around Poplar Point and Campsite #39 and then south of Long Island and into John Mack Bay. John Mack Landing is across the bay by Campsite #27. Enter a small cove and you can leave your canoe in the woods. The beginning of the trail is visible and well marked.

The trail is wide and well used and red trail markers are clearly visible. It has not been groomed recently, however, and there are currently a number of deadfalls that require short detours that are difficult only with a loaded pack frame. It is still a very easy 1.7-mile walk with a 195-foot climb to John Mack Pond. Even family groups with small children can make the walk in an hour.

The path forks at a sign showing Long Pond to the right. Take the left trail downhill to get to John Mack Pond. As you approach the pond there is a little-used path to the left toward some high ground along the north shore. If you take that path you will come to two campsites, one near the shore and the other up on the hill. If you are camping this is a good place to watch deer in the swamps on the south shore.

If you go straight ahead instead of going along the north shore you will find two boats which will float if the rainwater is bailed out. Paddles or oars must be improvised. The state stocks the pond with brook trout which can be seen rising to the surface in the evening. As you paddle toward the far shore a beaver will set off an alarm by slapping the water with its tail. Blueberry bushes grow around almost all the shoreline of the pond. In early June wildflowers, including pink lady's-slippers, are plentiful.

There is another campsite for a small tent just west of the boats toward the exit of the pond. A barred owl will hoot you to sleep and you will be awakened by the quack of a duck feeding in the bay. A trip to the pond makes a good addition to a camping vacation along Indian Lake. It is also a relatively easy overnight backpacking trip.

56 Long Pond from John Mack Pond

Trail, fishing, camping, swimming
2 miles, 1½ hours, minimal vertical rise

Long Pond has always been accessible to sportsmen from the south (see section 38). The state trail to Long Pond from John Mack Pond on the north, however, has received sporadic maintenance. At present, you can still follow the red trail markers, but almost no foot tread survives. If the trail is cleared, it would make a good through route, but the tall witch hobble and current beaver flooding make attempting it quite questionable. The following details are useful, only if some clearing is done.

As you hike in from Indian Lake (section 55), 100 yards west of John Mack Pond a sign indicates that Long Pond is 2.05 miles distant. The trail heads south towards the outlet of John Mack Pond. When you reach the outlet the trail markers lead you into water which looks three to four feet deep. Seventy-five feet from the trail, downstream to the right, the beavers have constructed an extensive dam and it is possible to walk across it without too much difficulty. The trail then skirts the pond's south side.

After walking for thirty minutes you will see a beaver flow through the trees on the northeast. Another five minutes of walking will bring you to an extensive former beaver works of considerable size. There are several tiers of ponds with the lodge, apparently deserted, in the second tier. The trail is along the steep hill on the south side of the pond but it is not clear and some markers are missing. If you stay low on this hillside along the flow you will reach the small stream that feeds it. At this point, the trail, with its markers, reappears.

Crotched Pond

The trail winds back and forth across a small stream three times in the next five minutes of walking. Another five-minute walk will bring you to an extremely large beaver flow. There are numerous signs of current beaver dam construction but the outlet is narrow and there are two possible places to cross if one uses a hiking stick for balance. Any additional beaver works here should stabilize the dams and improve the crossing. The trail is easily picked up on the other side of the water, going toward high ground on Long Pond Ridge.

The trail now follows the old roadbed as it curves north of east around the ridge, and then circles around the end of the ridge on high ground to head south again. After the trail turns south, it is a twenty-minute walk to the northwestern corner of Long Pond. The route continues as a path along the western side of Long Pond. Follow it south until you pass the rocky peninsula that juts into the pond and then turn east across a swampy area to the point. It is only a twenty-minute walk along the shore to that promontory, which is the best place to camp, swim, or picnic.

Long Pond has been well used in the past few years and spring and summer will usually find fishermen or camping groups there.

The walk from the John Mack Landing on Indian Lake is 3.7 miles along and will take over two and a half hours, one way. Even though the markings persist, the flooding from new beaver work and the numerous saplings filling the route make this currently a very difficult trail to follow.

57 Crotched Pond from Indian Lake
Old road, campsites, fishing

There are two routes to Crotched Pond, one from Indian Lake and one from Big Brook Road (section 66). If you can manage the peculiar transportation problems, with a boat at one end and a car at the other, you can combine both routes to make a through walk past the pond.

The recent state acquisition of almost all of the shoreline of Crotched Pond and a huge tract surrounding it open exciting new camping opportunities to the public. The spruce-bordered pond is home to loons, mergansers, and ducks. Only a small portion of the northeast shore is private and off-limits, but unfortunately that shore includes the long peninsula that is the easiest point to reach along the shoreline.

The path to Crotched Pond begins behind Campsite #14 on the east shore of Indian Lake, and is accessible only by water. Getting your canoe to the water on the west shore of Indian Lake in the general area of the path is difficult since that shoreline is either privately owned or, where it is state-owned Forest Preserve, the lake is a considerable distance from the road. It is only a thirty-minute paddle across the lake from Sabael, if you have permission to put in where NY 30 is close to the lake. The other launching is to put in just south of Poplar Point where the road again approaches the lake but this requires about a 1½-hour paddle. It is a beautiful lake with an attractive distant view of the High Peaks to the north, so the paddle is enjoyable unless you are bucking a stiff wind.

Campsite #14 is opposite the south tip of Crotched Pond Island. Paddle around to the right where there is a little cove with a small beach. You can hide your canoe and paddles in the woods. You will easily spot the path about 10 yards in from the beach.

The path, which is unmarked but well traveled, heads inland on an abandoned logging road and almost immediately crosses the wide, stony bed of Crotched Pond Brook. Because the roadway on the right, or south, side of the brook is often fairly muddy, hikers have worn a new path on higher ground a few feet away; it makes better walking than the main path.

After ten minutes of walking you will pass a lovely small cascade. Beyond it the path recrosses the brook in a very boggy area. You will have to look hard to pick up the path in the high grass on the brook's north side, but keep walking up beside the brook and you will find it. Soon you will see a very substantial beaver dam on the right. The dam is three or four feet high and creates a large pond. It is a good place for a picture. The path is on the side hill so the pond does not interfere with hiking.

Beyond the beaver dam, the path gradually leaves the brook and continues in deep forest. Beyond a gentle rise to a height-of-land, you descend and pass a small swampy area on the right that is full of Labrador Tea and other plants that like to grow with their roots wet. The path is quite wide here as it was used by ATVs up to the time of the sale to the state.

After walking for a total of forty minutes, you head up a slight hill through stands of raspberries that thrive in the logged lands. Beyond is a grassy clearing and a path forks right from it to the pond. This point is very difficult to spot. It led to a campsite that used to be the only part of the pond owned by the state. The logging road continues west, before branching to the still privately owned peninsula. The state now owns all the land from a point west of the peninsula all the way back around the pond.

Crotched Pond is an unusually lovely body of water with many bays and stumps and water lilies, but no sandy beach for swimming. It is quite large (57 acres) and stocked with brook trout. It is a marvelous place to have a boat for fishing or for exploring its sinuous shoreline and the outlet marshes. The pond is nestled at 1820 feet elevation, overlooked by Crotched Mountain, which rises 950 feet to the east, and Kunjamuk Mountain, which is 1100 feet above it on the southeast. Both of those mountains are now state-owned and the latter has a series of intriguing cliffs and much open rock on its fire-scarred southern slopes.

If you want to bring an inflatable boat to the lake, it is easier to approach it from the east and Big Brook Road (see section 66).

58 Baldface Mountain

Trail, spectacular views
1.3 miles, 1¹/₄ hours round trip after a canoe trip, 580-foot climb

Baldface is a friendly mountain with a magnificent view of Indian Lake and its bordering mountains. With a vertical rise of only 580 feet to its 2230-foot summit, it can easily be climbed by almost everyone.

The trailhead, which is accessible only by water, is on the eastern shore of Normans Cove (section 52). Boats can be pulled up on the beach beside a rock painted with a faint white circle. The trail, along which yellow DEC trail markers have been posted, starts inland from the rock.

The route is wide and well defined and climbs gently at first through second growth woods, following for a time an intermittent streambed.

Partway up the slope, the trail enters an area of much larger trees, with many giant maples, birch, and beech. As it winds upwards, the trail heads through a small draw, where you can begin to see the cliffs of Baldface ranging on your left. After you climb up the valley and cross the dry streambed, follow the trail around to the left up a short steep pitch on to the ridge. It circles the cliffs, approaching them from the east. As the trail climbs the ridge, it bends to the right through the evergreens to the rocky summit.

Several vantages crown the cliffs and the views are spectacular. Indian Lake spreads out below you with almost all of its fourteen-mile length and two dozen islands visible. You can look up the Jessup River to the south. Snowy, with its fire tower, and Panther, Squaw, Porter, and Burgess mountains range across the lake, while in the distant northwest rises the scarred hulk of Blue Mountain. New young trees are beginning to crowd the view to the north, which includes a part of the High Peaks. Few mountains offer such a fine panorama for the little effort needed to reach the summit.

59 Lake Abanakee

Canoeing

Some twenty-five years ago, the Indian River was dammed 4 miles below its origin at the Indian Lake Dam. This dam created Lake Abanakee, a shallow lake ideal for short, easy canoe trips. It offers lots of variety and fairly good protection from the winds.

The best place to launch your canoe or kayak is from the parking lot east of the causeway on which Big Brook Road crosses the lake. Big Brook Road heads southeast from NY 30 a little over 0.5 mile south of Indian Lake village. There is a second launching spot on Jerry Savarie Road, a right, or south, turn past the parking area. If you use this second spot, launch near the bridge on that road.

To explore the section of the lake toward the Indian Lake Dam, paddle southwest past a campground on a handsome cedar bank. You will pass the Jerry Savarie Road bridge that spans Big Brook. Turn right and after passing a row of camps you reach open, shallow water, which is often the haunt of young ducks and mergansers. The lake narrows, and you really are in the Indian River. It is not possible to canoe to the rapids below the big Indian Lake Dam without a portage. Since this area is the best and most secluded part of the trip, you may want to pull your canoe on shore to the right of the first large rapids, where there is a path you can use to portage your canoe to deep water, where it can be launched again. The series of rapids and pools up to the dam are in a deep valley, mostly untouched by nearby civilization.

When you return and put in your canoe north of the rapids again, paddle along the opposite bank, where you will see a small hermit camp on private land. The total time for the round trip from the parking area to the rapids is about one hour; allow more time if you wish to portage above them.

If you want to explore further, carry your canoe across Big Brook Road where you parked and put in on the other side. There is a bridge beneath the road, but engineers did not have canoeists in mind when they built the causeway. Paddle north. Beyond some camps and a point of land, the lake narrows to the old river channel for a few hundred yards and then opens out again. You will see several small islands before you come to an open area from which NY 28 traffic is visible.

It is possible to paddle to the NY 28 bridge; a trip from the causeway to the bridge takes about forty-five minutes.

To extend a day of paddling, you might wish to venture into the narrow channels of Big Brook. To reach the brook, just paddle under the Jerry Savarie Road bridge. If you take the middle channel it leads into the narrow stream of Big Brook and winds through alder thickets and rocky ledges. The road is close and the brook actually passes several backyards before reaching a pool with two impossible ledges upstream, the end of the navigable water.

If you stay to the left on the return and cross the open water, full of stumps, you will enter another stream, Round Pond Brook. That brook wanders toward the south, getting shallower as it goes. Be careful to avoid the numerous boulders. There are several small ledges that require portages and finally a beaver dam that you would have to cross to explore the small pond on the other side.

Both brooks offer short yet beautiful paddles. The shores of the lake are lovely, and if you combine all the routes, you can have an easy and rewarding day on the water.

Near The Old Wilderness Lodge

IN THE 1860s, a string of small communities dotted the area east of Big Brook Road, south of Indian Lake village. Each clustered around a sawmill, a store, or a hotel. A sawmill operated by John Eldridge on Center Brook was the nucleus of one of these settlements. Eldridge was a lumberman and the grandfather of William Waddell, who contributed many of this guide's historical notes about old logging days in the Siamese Ponds Wilderness Area.

One of the communities north of Center Brook was called Little Canada, for all the loggers who immigrated from Canada to harvest timber in the nineteenth century. Many of the area's early residents were Canadian.

In the late 1930s, a resort, Wilderness Lodge, was built on the site of the Eldridge mill. In the last decade, a modern development has sprung up around the old resort, and the lodge is once again serving guests. The old mill pond on Center Creek has been enlarged to become Rainbow Lake.

To the northeast of Rainbow Lake three very special small ponds surround an unusual hill; you surely will want to visit them. However, the ponds are accessible only from roads in the new development, which is not shown on the current USGS map. The roads are sufficiently confusing that the best introduction to the area is a description of them and the accesses they provide to the paths and trails leading to the ponds.

Drive south on Big Brook Road for 1.8 miles beyond the end of the causeway across Abanakee Lake. Immediately beyond the Chimney Mountain Craftsmen furniture mill, Big Brook Road bears right or south; take a left turn toward Wilderness Lodge (there is a sign) and the development of vacation homes. A few hundred yards in, the road forks and you go left, on Starbuck Road, which comes to a T 1.2 miles from Big Brook Road. A left turn at the T takes you in 0.25 mile to the parking area for the John Pond Trail (section 62). A right at the T takes you to a dead end where the narrow path for Clear Pond begins (section 61). Look for this path on the right side at the very end of the road. Backtracking from the T for 0.25 mile and turning north on a narrower dirt road takes you in about 180 yards to the beginning of the path to Center Pond (section 60). The path begins from a small parking turnout just before the road reaches a camp.

60 Center Pond
Short path, fishing

The average hiker may ignore Center Pond, but fishermen and naturalists will enjoy this swampy little pond. From the beginning of the path described in the chapter introduction, it is a short walk—no more than 300 steps—to the pond.

Walking the shores is impossible, and the pond is partially filled with reeds and grasses. It has been stocked with brook trout and it would certainly be easier to enjoy fishing or exploring for unusual plants if you had a boat. The short path makes an easy carry possible. As at many other interior Adirondack ponds, there is an old rowboat here.

61 Clear Pond
Path, campsite, fishing

Set between small hills with white birch and a few old pines around its shore, Clear Pond is truly lovely. There are many campsites, mostly used by fishermen, and the pond has been stocked with brook trout. Several sites have places to swim nearby, and a fairly good path winds around the north and east sides of the pond.

The path to Clear Pond is well defined and well used, although its entrance into the woods is unmarked. Its beginning, described in the introduction, is almost concealed.

The path makes a mile-long curve to the northeast around a ridge. Note that the path does not follow the trail designated on the most recent USGS map. The new route climbs barely 200 feet around the shoulder of the ridge, wandering up and down through a tall, handsome forest. It then descends to the outlet, which has been flooded by beaver. Cross the outlet below the beaver dam and discover a path that hugs the northern and eastern shores, passing several nice campsites. The path peters out before reaching the southeast corner, which also has been flooded by beaver.

If you can circle those eastern beaver marshes, you will have only a short, additional 0.5-mile bushwhack due south through fairly open woods to the northern end of John Pond. The bushwhack climbs little more than 100 feet over the low shoulder that separates the ponds. Given that the route to John Pond (section 61) remains a mess, this is certainly the most

pleasant and shortest way to reach that pond, even if there is no trail or path for part of the trip.

Clear Pond is the prettiest of the three little ponds in the Big Brook drainage, with water lilies in the shallows and clumps of the crested fern *Dryopteris cristata* dotting its shores. The mountain rising to the southeast is part of Bullhead. The 1-mile walk to the pond takes little more than a half hour, so this could be an easy camping trip, or part of a longer bushwhack to John Pond via the ridge south of Clear Pond.

62 John Pond

Trail, fishing, camping, cross-country skiing
2.8 miles one way, 1¹/₄ hours, minimal vertical rise

There are blue hiking trail markers along the route to John Pond, which begins from the parking area described in the chapter introduction. Another hiking and ski-touring trail branches off from it leading to Puffer Pond (section 70) and from there to the Old Farm Clearing south of Thirteenth Lake (section 86). The John Pond Trail is in a Wilderness Area, but in spite of the fact that the Unit Management Plan calls for limiting vehicular use on the access road, there are no barriers, few Wilderness signs, and little to deter those who have driven the road and make it muddy and rutted. A walk along this road can be depressing.

The road is now officially closed east of a point a little over a mile from the pond where there is a small, very old cemetery at the end of a path that leads 100 yards north from the road/trail. A parking area will be constructed nearby and when barriers are in place, the last portion of the hike will gradually improve. The western 1.7 miles will not be barred to traffic. Vehicular use, or abuse, has not only made the western portion of the road unpleasant for hiking, it has made such large ruts and mud wallows that only a few high-wheel-based trucks can negotiate the road.

Nevertheless, John Pond is quite handsome, fairly shallow, and stocked with brook trout. An exposed ridgeline marks the hill northwest of the pond, and there are good views from its prominent cliffs.

At the parking area 0.25 mile south of the T, a registration booth marks the beginning of the road/trail. Plowing ends at this point, so this marks

View West from Long Pond Ridge

the beginning of a pleasant ski trip even if the beginning, as a hike, is less than pleasant. Mudholes quickly make the trail impassible to vehicles, or at least it appears that way.

The road borders marshes as it heads south. After almost a mile, where the road takes a sharp bend to the east, a path straight ahead leads into a big meadow beside the brook where there is a campsite beneath old apple trees. For the next 0.8 mile, the roadway/trail continues to border the meadow, offering glimpses through the trees of mountains to the south. At one point you have a glimpse of the Chimney on Chimney Mountain. At a second unmarked fork, a right turn leads to a long meadow along the brook with an especially fine view of Bullhead Mountain. Skiers may want to improvise a loop through these flats south of the road to enhance their ski trip.

The road crosses the Hamilton-Warren County line 1.7 miles from the start, not far from where the new parking area will be built. The road is barred at this point and if the town maintains the road up to this point, a summer trek to John Pond will be shortened to just over a mile.

The road now enters a reforestation area. A short distance into it, look for the small path that forks left to the cemetery, which is the excuse given for the use of motorized vehicles so far into this Wilderness Area.

The road remains level as you leave the brook. Just before the road starts to rise, notice the blue trail markers and yellow ski-touring signs on the trail heading south down a small draw, across a field, then over the brook. This is the state trail to Puffer Pond (section 70).

Just beyond this fork, the road/trail begins to rise, still in the handsome reforestation area. Almost immediately you cross John Pond outlet and have an easy fifteen-minute walk left to reach the pond.

The entire walk to John Pond is so level that it would be a delight were it not for the mud holes. It makes an excellent ski-touring route and winter visitors often surprise small herds of wintering deer along the trail.

The trail reaches the south end of John Pond beside the state lean-to. There are other informal campsites around the pond. The deep hemlock woods to the east have lovely ground covers, including pipsissiwa, which blooms in mid-July. You will also find a variety of bladderworts around the edges of the pond.

63 Cliffs on John Pond Ridge

Two moderate bushwhacks

A climb to the cliffs on the John Pond Ridge to enjoy the fantastic views can be combined with walks to Clear and John ponds to create a great loop for a full-day hike. There are actually a series of cliffs on the ridge, all less than 500 feet above the pond and facing southeast. The views from them extend more than 180 degrees from north to south; but openings to the west and northwest from other points on the ridge extend the panorama to every point on the compass.

Two different approaches to the ridge are given here; both are good and both are loops. The first involves a visit to both ponds and suggests two possible routes up the ridge itself.

Walk to John Pond (section 62) and bushwhack around its west side for 150 to 200 yards to a deep gully up the side of the ridge. Follow the gully, which turns south, until you reach a point where the climb to the top of the ledges looks reasonable. This will bring you to the south end of the ledges, and as you make your way along to the northernmost ledges, the view will change spectacularly.

From the southernmost vantage point, the view is south, east, and west, with Bullhead Mountain looming large in front. This is one of the few places from which the chimney of Chimney Mountain can be seen. Beyond Chimney are Puffer, Humphrey, and Horseshoe mountains. To the west is the whole Indian Lake range.

There is a ravine to the north, between this ledge and the next, in the middle part of the ridge, which is 150 feet higher. The climb to it gets very steep toward the top, where you mount a narrow rock ridge as sharp as a knife edge. Once on top, birches glisten against the open rock faces. John Pond lies below and the view includes Peaked, Slide, Ruby, Davis, Starbuck, Casey, Bell, and Vanderwhacker mountains and the High Peaks in the distant northeast.

An alternate climb from John Pond to the middle ridge involves using an unusual rock ledge that traverses the face of these cliffs at a very steep angle. To reach it, walk almost to the northwest corner of the pond. From the lean-to at the southeast corner of the pond, it is as easy to walk along the eastern edge of the pond as the west to reach this point, and the west side has the advantage of views up to the ledges you are about to climb.

At the summit, about 200 yards north of the crest of the middle ridge, you can find open rock slides facing west. From these openings you can see

Blue Mountain beyond Indian Lake, with Lake Abanakee, Rainbow Flow, Center Ponds, and the range of hills at the north end of Indian Lake in the foreground.

To the north, a third crest on the ridge also has open ledges below the summit. It is separated from the middle hump by a small ravine.

The range of open rock beyond the last summit makes a gentle downward arc to the east. Follow the open places, descending about 100 feet, then bushwhack almost due north to Clear Pond. It is easy to walk along the southwestern shore to the northwestern tip of the pond and the path there (section 61). The bushwhack between the two ponds via the ridge is approximately 1 mile long and requires a little over two hours. Take binoculars and stop often to enjoy the view. The entire loop makes a full day's adventure.

The second, shorter loop involves walking first to Clear Pond (section 61). This takes just over a half hour. Continue along the faint path on the southwestern side of the pond for five minutes, then head uphill, due south, for a short, steep ascent to the chain of open rock areas. Your first view along the ridge toward the south emphasizes the narrow spine of the arc of the ridge. The cliffs sheathing the hill are like the vertical armor of a giant stegosaurus that has curled around John Pond.

Walk south to the middle of the ridge and the highest peak. From this point it is very easy to complete the bushwhack directly back to the beginning of the path to Clear Pond. Make the steep ascent down the south end of the middle ridge and walk southwest around a small knoll. Keep to a level contour around it, heading generally west, then a little north of west. The top of the knoll has many long parallel rock ridges, which are characteristic of the area. A half-hour walk from the ridge should put you right back at your car. The bushwhack is through a very handsome, open, hardwood forest with significant clumps of birch.

This entire loop is over 3 miles long and can be walked in a little over two hours, but you are certain to find so much to see that even four hours will be inadequate for the trip.

The Northern Kunjamuk Road

IN THE NINETEENTH century, the Kunjamuk Road was a major north-south "highway" from Speculator to Indian Lake. In the far north it followed the route of the present Big Brook Road. That road forks southeast from NY 30, 0.5 mile south of Indian Lake village.

One hundred years ago the section of the Kunjamuk Road, from Round Pond to where it today intersects Big Brook Road, followed a different route. According to the USGS map issued in 1890, the Kunjamuk Road headed west from Big Brook Road across a bridge north of the present Kings Flow dam. The 0.7-mile section from there followed approximately the route indicated on the 1954 map, except that the 1954 map shows the road beginning at the dam rather than at Big Brook Road. Good trackers can still see traces of the overgrown roadway and historically minded bushwhackers might wish to try to find it.

At present, however, the easiest way to begin to follow the Kunjamuk Road from the north is to walk to Round Pond on one of International Paper Company's logging roads (section 64). IP does not now require a permit for those who use the Crotched Pond area.

64 Round Pond from Big Brook Road
Logging road, fishing, camping

Round Pond is a very handsome body of water, but the principal walking route to the pond is far from pretty. However, you will want to use it if you plan to camp at Round Pond or if you are going to walk south on the Kunjamuk Road.

The route to Round Pond follows a logging road through International Paper Company's land. To reach it, follow the Big Brook Road for 5 miles from the Lake Abanakee causeway south to a right turn, southwest. Immediately after turning off Big Brook Road the logging road crosses Round Pond Brook on a good bridge. However, it is better to park on the Big Brook Road side of the bridge where there is room for several cars.

Follow the logging road southwest for 300 yards to a junction. The road toward Crotched Pond (section 66) continues straight; the road to Round Pond forks left, south. The area has been logged, removing the canopy over the roadway and creating a number of side roads. The more obvious route is always the correct one; two right forks at first, then a left where the right leads uphill. The roadway is distinctly rutted and muddy. Taking the next right turn, a pitch up over a stretch of road worn to bare rock leads to a Wilderness Area sign. The roadway drops less than 50 feet as it approaches Round Pond. The 2-mile walk to the pond is a 200-foot climb and takes forty minutes.

Round Pond with Puffer Mountain in the background

Round Pond lies entirely on state land, and it is always a pleasant surprise after the walk through the logged woods. It has sandy shores and birch-covered banks. You're apt to startle a pair of loons. The road continues southwest beside the lake, but never far from it. Humphrey Mountain is visible to the south, and the cliffs on the hill northwest of Chimney Mountain can be seen in the north. From a vantage 0.3 mile southwest along the shore, you can see almost all of the west side of Puffer Mountain; it is a marvelous place to appreciate just how steep Puffer is.

Rainbow trout have been stocked in the pond and spring fishing has been good there in past years. A site near the point the road first approaches the pond has been used for camping, but it is so impacted and close to water, camping is prohibited here.

There is a path of sorts around the north and northeast sides of Round Pond that at one time connected with routes to Kings Flow. Whether following it or bushwhacking, it is not difficult to traverse the northeast shore with its tall hemlock and spruce and occasionally dense understory of witch hobble and small evergreens. There is a campsite near the outlet on the eastern shore.

65 The Kunjamuk Road from the North
Old road, path, ski-touring

South of Round Pond, the path along the Kunjamuk Road follows exactly the route laid out almost 150 years ago. Walk to Round Pond (section 64) and along its shore and the marshy southern end of the pond with its huge mud flats. At just short of 3 miles from Big Brook Road, the roadway jogs right toward a cabin. Straight ahead leads into a wallow, so jog right and quickly left to continue south around the wallow.

Marshes continue off to your left and the road/trail is flat and rutted. Twenty-five minutes from the cabin, at just over 4 miles, you cross a stream. Just beyond, a yellow ribbon marks a path to the left that hunters use to reach the high pass between Crotched Pond Mountain and Kunjamuk Mountain. Still flat and quite muddy, the trail continues with marshes visible through the trees to the east. You can see the cliffs on Pine Peak above these marshes.

Soon you begin to see marshes off to your right as well, some with open water. Just after you cross a minor drainage that flows from your right, watch for yellow and orange markers on a tree. These mark the end of the skiers' flagged path from Long Pond. This point is nearly 5 miles from Big Brook Road and you can walk it in just under two hours, probably quicker than whatever is making the wheel ruts that continue to disturb the trail. The reason for the ruts becomes obvious ten minutes later when you pass a clearing with the frame of a hunters camp—its remains standing illegally in this wilderness area.

Another stream flows from the marshes to the right, west of the trail, which has become very narrow and not all that obvious. You pick up red flagging to help you through. Twenty-five minutes from the flagged route, at about 6 miles, you reach Wakeley Brook. The path forks; the right leads to a beaver dam that detours you across the flooded brook. However, downstream dams are washed out enough so that a crossing via the left path is quite easy. It follows the continuing roadway.

Across the brook the trail heads gently uphill for its 2.4- mile circuit of the eastern and southern flanks of Petes Hill. This stretch is quite overgrown and would be hard to follow were it not for the red flagging. A spectacular forest of tall hardwoods rims the hill—the big maples give a primeval feeling to the place. Huge fields of maidenhair fern fill the understory and conceal the roadway—they would be exceptionally beautiful if they were not laced with horse nettles. Rattlesnake and Goldies ferns complete the mosaic underfoot.

At one point, Humphrey Mountain is visible above the marshes and open water to the east. An enormous field of horse nettles covers the whole hillside just before the road reenters deep woods and becomes much easier to follow. The road has headed southwest across a height-of-land, then begins to descend along a long, thin ridge. Nearly 2 miles from Wakeley Brook, a fifty-minute walk, watch for red flagging to the right. It marks a route that has no foot tread, but leads northwest, directly down to a branch of the Kunjamuk. This route is above the marshes and flooded area that make it impossible to follow the roadway across the river. If you want to continue on the road, something that is often possible when the marshes are frozen, you descend the ridge into a lovely pine stand. The road sort of disappears as it approaches a tributary of the Kunjamuk that comes in from the east. Walk slightly right, out onto the marshes. The tall pines across the water mark the western end of the road, which seems tantalizingly close. Unless the beaver dams are washed out or frozen or else the marsh is dry enough so you can reach the dams to use them as bridges to cross the flooded marshes, you will have to go back and use the flagged route to intercept the continuation of the Kunjamuk Road.

If you follow the flags, they lead downhill to a deep valley where the river is nothing more than a narrow stream with more than enough rocks for an easy crossing. However, you will find that after crossing this northern tributary of the Kunjamuk, the flags still lead you into a very wet spruce bog. The route eventually curves south, paralleling the marshes. It intersects the roadway about 100 yards south of the point where the Kunjamuk Road enters the marsh from the south. Once back on the Kunjamuk Road, you are but five minutes northeast of the fork to Rock Pond (section 37).

A note about the flagged route north of Long Pond Mountain: the UMP recommended that such a route be cut, but the flagging is informal and possibly illegal. It is used extensively by guided groups skiing from lodge to lodge—probably the safest way to enjoy the route—and a cleared path of sorts exists. The route heads east toward an open marsh that is less than five minutes from the Kunjamuk Road. It angles right through the marsh, then curves around the northern flanks of Long Pond Mountain before heading south along them, then heads west in a series of steps that take it to a northern draw on Long Pond. No flagging is visible from the pond. If you wish to walk from west to east, look for the path in the northeast corner. It heads up through a small marsh—no place to walk in summer!— and continues beside a small brook into the notch above. It is a hard 1.3-mile walk from the road to the pond. If you lose the flagged route you could end up in one of the ubiquitous boggy hollows that make walking off the trail anywhere in this region almost impossible.

You can also use the Kunjamuk Road as a jumping off point for the Long Pond Cliffs. Any bushwhack you choose will involve a fair amount of spruce thickets, but the route that appears to encounter the fewest obstacles takes off from the Kunjamuk Road just south of the small stream, which in turn is immediately south of the beginning of the flagged ski route, 5.5 miles from Round Pond. A bushwhack to the southwest, seeking high ground and avoiding most of the spruce bogs, leads to the northern end of the small hill with the cliffs in forty-five minutes (see section 39).

Any accessible portion of this road makes great cross-country skiing. Because the Kunjamuk Road is not plowed through IP's Speculator Tree Farm, a through route is 18 miles long, too strenuous for all but the strongest skiers. It is suitable for a winter camping trip and outfitters have in recent years guided groups along this route, leading them on a true wilderness experience. The safest way to enjoy a through ski trip is certainly with such a group.

66 Crotched Pond from Big Brook Road
Logging roads

To reach Crotched Pond from the north and east, drive south on Big Brook Road for 5 miles from the causeway over Lake Abanakee to the lumber road that heads west into International Paper Company land. Park before the Big Brook bridge (see section 64). The Crotched Pond Tract is still open to the public and there is no permit system here at present. IP is continuing its practice of leasing building sites to groups for camps, and the leases give rights only to the land on which the camps are built. It is possible, however, that IP will sell exclusive leases to portions of the Crotched Pond Tract in the future. At present, access is not limited, but fires and camping are prohibited.

The tract is not being logged at present, but there remains a confusion of skid trails from the last logging. Extensive vehicular traffic on the main route to the newly created private inholding on Crotched Pond (section 57) should make the way quite obvious.

Follow the road west. After five minutes you will reach the left fork that heads south to Round Pond. Keep right for Crotched Pond. After a fifteen-minute walk, you reach another fork; again keep to the right. The walking is easy and there are several clearings made by the logging operations. These soon disappear and the road climbs gently through deeper woods; the road is curving south as you reach a height-of-land after an hour and twenty minutes.

The road then drops fairly quickly and almost due south into the Crotched Pond valley. The main road you are following leads directly to the camp on the peninsula (section 57). As the road levels out, you will notice a right, west, fork, which is the trail to Indian Lake.

It takes less than two hours to walk the 4.5-mile distance from Big Brook Road to the pond, short enough for a day hike and one that can be extended to Indian Lake. While the walking is easy on the logging roads, be prepared for the fact there are no markers on them. Take a compass, for you may find yourself making a wrong turn and walking in a direction opposite your destination.

Kings Flow Trailhead

ON THE EAST side of Indian Lake, at the end of Big Brook Road, there is a private lake formed by the damming of a large swamp that surrounded a much smaller lake. For a time, the owners changed the name of the newly created lake to Lake Humphrey, but at present the shallow lake is known by its original name, which derived from the King family.

The King family logged the Puffer Mountain and Humphrey Mountain areas, living for a time in a camp at the foot of Humphrey. Before the turn of the century, they built a log dam on Wakely Brook for the spring run near the site of the present dam. The Kings farmed the fields at the north end of the flow from the late 1800s through the early 1900s. Descendants of the first farmer recall visits by traveling peddlers who walked the Kunjamuk Road north from Speculator. Most of the property was sold to the state. A scout camp was located at the north end of the flow.

Recently, the Kings Flow Scout Camp and all the land at the north end of the flow have been sold to a private group. At present, they continue the camp's policy of permitting parking in the fields at the head of the flow. For a modest fee ($1 per car) you can park and walk to the state trails to Chimney Mountain and Puffer Pond. No camping, hunting, or fishing is permitted on the private lands. Because the group plans to rent the cabins during summer months, they wish to protect their rights to the water. Hence, there is no general access to the trails to the south (sections 68, 71, and 72). You may request permission to cross the private lands to intersect these routes. Please, do respect this private property. The group's experience in granting access has not been all positive and it would be a shame if the activities of a few meant that access for all were denied.

For reasons of liability, no one is allowed to cross the outlet dam. Because of this and because the scouts are no longer there to mark the routes on the west side of the flow through Round Pond, this access to the south is much less easy to follow than in previous years.

67 Chimney Mountain
Trail, caves, views
1 mile one way, ¾ hour, 900-foot climb

Without proper introduction, the 900-foot climb along the 1 mile of well-used path to Chimney Mountain might sound like an ordinary adventure. However, this small mountain is unique in the Adirondacks. Exploring it is an experience you will not forget; it is certain that climbing it once will not suffice.

GEOLOGIC BACKGROUND

The western face of the mountain has pulled away, opening a small rift valley. As you approach the end of the climb to the rift, you will begin to see huge blocks of rock scattered and heaped into piles. Travel over the rocks in the rift is difficult and progress can be rather slow.

When you first enter this cleft you will be amazed by the stark outline of the "Chimney" silhouetted against the skyline at the northern end. The silence of the small valley is overwhelming; its sheer walls will make you feel totally isolated.

The starkness of the rock faces will also make you wonder how recent the cataclysmic events were that shaped the rift. You will certainly be awed by the evidence of the great geologic forces that created this unusual rock formation.

Your introduction to the mountain starts with the ancient rocks that make up the Adirondacks. Beginning about 2.3 billion years ago, limestone and sandstone sediments were deposited in an area known as the Grenville Sea, a shallow body of water. Slowly, throughout the Precambrian period, sediments accumulated in the sea until about 1.4 billion years ago.

In the next 200 million years, a period of mountain building known as the Grenville orogeny occurred. Some speculate that the orogeny was caused by the collision of continental plates. Whatever the reason, the event changed all the area's rocks. The sediments were intruded by magma, which cooled into syenite, gabbro, and granite. The entire mass lay several miles below the surface of the earth and the resulting heat and pressures metamorphosed any rocks that predated the Grenville Sea as

Exploring for caves on Chimney Mountain

well as the sediments and intrusions. The metamorphism deformed the various layers and produced syenite gneiss, granite gneiss, and metagabbro. Erosion gradually took away the overburden, bringing to the surface these rocks which make up some Adirondack mountains. About 400 million years ago, another period of upheaval created faults in the rock mass and expansion of the eroded layers created other faults.

When the last layer of resistant rock covering Chimney Mountain was worn away, an upturned sandwich of syenite gneiss, metamorphosed Grenville sediments or marbles, and a topping of layered granite gneiss was exposed. Erosion of the exposed surfaces was most rapid in the relatively softer middle layer; and, as the top was undercut, a huge triangular block broke away, creating the rift on the mountain. Smaller blocks were moved along the fracture zones by ice and by the collapse of the triangular block, creating caves in the rift and in its western wall.

How gentle and benign are the contours of our Adirondacks in contrast with their turbulent past! Nowhere are the events that shaped the ancient rocks into mountains as fresh as on Chimney Mountain. If, as geologists have speculated, the events that created the magnificent rift occurred as recently as the retreat of the last glacier, then geologically it is as if the event happened yesterday.

The rift is over 600 feet long and between 150 and 200 feet deep. It ranges in width up to 250 feet. The marvelous rock column, the Chimney, that gave its name to the mountain towers 35 feet above the east wall of the rift. A smaller carbon-copy of the Chimney rests partially concealed by trees, in a pile of rubble 400 feet west northwest of the Chimney. The valley and the northwest flank of the mountain are a jumble of huge blocks and slabs of the Grenville rock.

On opposite walls of the rift, identical layers of gneisses, quartzite, and mixed rocks can be traced, though the angle of the layers is much steeper on the eastern face.

Fractures in the rocks have created many caves, some within the rift valley itself and some within the walls. The caves are so deep that ice appears to persist in them throughout the year, and it is even possible to find ice in some of the smaller ones in the valley as late as mid-July. Some of these caves can safely be explored by agile hikers, but there are also huge rooms and long passages that must be left to expert spelunkers.

It is enough for me to imagine what lies below as I stand on the west face of the rift enjoying the distant views. "An impressive chamber at the 150-foot level retains subfreezing temperatures into mid-October and ice over five feet thick through October." Eagle Cave, as named by its explorers, is the deepest and most spectacular cave discovered in the Adirondacks.

The Chimney

CHIMNEY MOUNTAIN

The accompanying map is designed to locate some of the major features. A few of the caves and crevices require no more than a flashlight and a hard hat to inspect. Others are for experts only, with spelunking and rock climbing equipment. On every visit to the area, I have discovered something new. The map was made with stereoscopic aerial photographs, altimeter, compass, and 100-foot tape, in an effort to make the sketch map of the previous edition more precise. It is still only an imperfect rendering of the area, but it should guide you to the more interesting features. There are many more caves and openings than indicated, so whenever walking in the area, be careful where you step.

View of Kings Flow from Chimney Mountain lookout

EXPLORING THE MOUNTAIN

Drive to the end of Big Brook Road to the camp of Kings Flow (see the introduction to Chapter VII—The Northern Kunjamuk Road). Signs at the camp point to the Chimney Mountain path, which begins east of the parking area in the northeast corner of the field. The ascent to the rift should take no more than forty-five minutes. The path heads northeast through deep wet woods, for a five-minute walk to a register booth beside a small stream. At first there is a bit of typical Adirondack mud underfoot. As the cover thins out to birch and witch hobble, notice what is happening underfoot. The trail becomes covered with sand that has eroded and washed from the Grenville layers above.

At the first lookout, the path forks. Follow either to loop through the rift and past the Chimney. If you choose to climb to the Chimney first and then into the rift to explore the caves, take the right fork to the east wall of the rift. Near the top you will notice a small ridge to the right, or east.

You will want to make a short detour and climb it for views east across the true summit of Chimney Mountain. On a clear day you can distinguish many of the High Peaks to the north as well as Bullhead and Puffer mountains to the east and southeast. Notice the Grenville blocks scattered through the valley between the ledge and the east summit. From this ledge it is a 0.3-mile bushwhack south of east to Chimney's true summit at 2721 feet. There are open patches along the way and more views, should you add this trek to your adventures.

Back on the path to the Chimney, climb west to the rock outcrops on the east wall of the rift, below the Chimney. If you walk carefully around to the north side of the Chimney you will find a window in the blocks of fallen rocks that frames an interesting view of the west wall. The ledges south of the Chimney are a good spot to stop and picnic and admire the rock spire. The many steps around the Chimney are deceptive; it should not be climbed without ropes and pitons. The west side of the Chimney is a nearly vertical wall 80 feet above the bottom of the rift.

To descend into the valley, walk back south along the path about 100 feet to find a small path that begins a steep descent into the rift. It is amazing how hot and dry and dusty the paths can be in summer. The drafts of cold air that emerge from deep within the cleft can be a pleasant contrast.

Walking through the rift can be dangerous. There are many informal paths that wind through the talus, but some of the holes between even small blocks are very deep. If the weather is warm, drafts of cold air will alert you to caves and crevices.

Some of the holes have a vertical drop of 80 feet and more, so do be careful, and especially watchful of small children. There are many more caves and openings than are shown on the accompanying map and many more than qualified explorers could discover in a half-dozen trips to the mountains.

Before leaving the valley, you may want to explore the broken rock that faces the north end of the rift where the most accessible cave will surely have ice in early July. For a spectacular view of the Chimney follow the informal path up the southwest side of the valley past the cave to the west wall. Walk north to the high point of the west wall for the Chimney view as well as the wonderful panorama of the High Peaks. An informal path leads south but gets mixed up in the maze of paths which have developed on the outer flanks of the west wall. You may have to bushwhack a bit to connect with the path that leads south to the main trail at just below the 2500-foot elevation point.

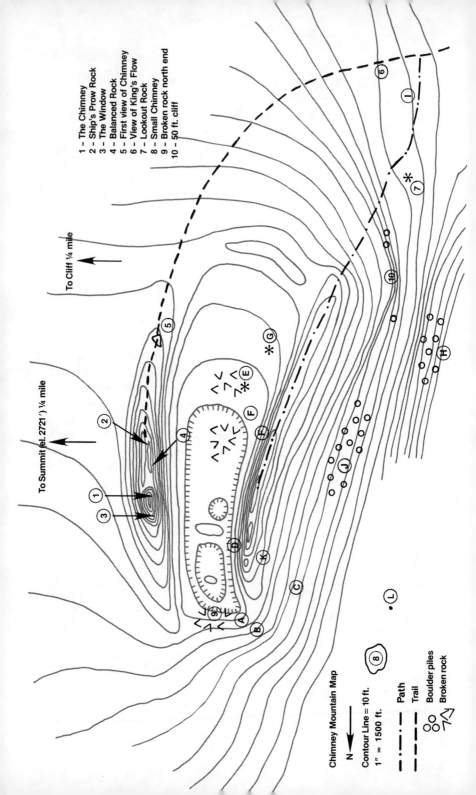

Chimney Mountain Map

1 – The Chimney
2 – Ship's Prow Rock
3 – The Window
4 – Balanced Rock
5 – First view of Chimney
6 – View of King's Flow
7 – Lookout Rock
8 – Small Chimney
9 – Broken rock north end
10 – 50 ft. cliff

To Cliff ¼ mile

To Summit (el. 2721') ¼ mile

N

Contour Line = 10 ft.
1″ = 1500 ft.

Path
Trail
Boulder piles
Broken rock

THE CAVES ON CHIMNEY MOUNTAIN

A. Cave part way up the low rock wall forming the north end of the rift. Hole about 3 feet in diameter goes down and curves west. May connect with B.

B. Opening about 50 feet below and near the north end of the west wall. Ropes are required to explore the several chambers.

C. Cave behind big boulder under an overhang near north end of west wall. Small rooms both to the left and right of the rock. The room on the right has ice in early summer; a hole in its floor is a source of cold air. May connect with B.

D. Cave with shaft entrance 5 feet high and 18 inches wide in the west wall. Runs parallel to the wall and then turns.

E. Spaces under big rock in the south central part of the rift.

F. Fairly accessible cave with three openings, one at the base of the cliff and two others partway up the west wall. There are three interconnected chambers, one of which looks into Eagle Cave.

G. The "ice" cave on Chimney; with the most accessible beginning. This cave usually has ice in mid-July. The opening in the ground by white birch leads down through broken rock to ice, though the first chamber may have dangerous loose rocks. Partially melted ice below reveals connections to four other chambers. This may be the cave discovered by Charles Carroll, proprietor of Chimney Mountain House at Lake Humphrey, now Kings Flow, in 1932. The series of horizontal and vertical passages below requires ropes.

H. The "Cavern" is a large room with a tunnel extending about 30 feet into the west wall of the ridge. No rope required; the cave is not deep. There are small side rooms filled with ice, and with a flashlight the passages are fairly easy to explore. The entrance is hard to find among the boulders.

I. Manhole-like opening to right of path about 150 feet from first view of Kings Flow. Rope required to explore the 70-foot-deep, four-level cave with ice.

J. Large crevasse, snow in mid-July, source of snowball fights.

K. "Eagle Cave" requires ropes and technical knowledge to explore. Entrance on side of ridge between two horizontal boulders. Deepest and most spectacular cave in the Adirondacks. Interconnecting caves underlie most of the entire west wall. Experts only.

L. Small cave located about 100 feet southwest of small chimney at base of small cliff.

68 Kings Flow

Path, old road, cross-country skiing, campsites

Only the northern end of Kings Flow is privately owned. A path follows an old logging road on state land along its eastern shore, providing a lovely short walk to the remote southern end of the flow. In spring enjoy it as a good, short nature trail; in winter use it as a ski-touring route; or in summer follow it to connecting paths that lead to adventures in the deep interior beyond the flow (sections 71–74).

With permission to cross the private lands, walk south through the field below the Kings Flow camps, across a bridge, and to the southeast corner of the next field. Here bear left onto the woods road which leads south through a scrub forest of small evergreens with lichens and mosses underfoot. Shortly, there is a stream crossing, with no bridge, and it can be a wet crossing in high water. Beyond is state land and the forest cover gradually increases in height. It is in this section that you will want to leave the path briefly and bushwhack to the flow for a view over its southern end and across to Humphrey Mountain.

After a thirty-minute walk, a bit over a mile, look for a V in the trail. A yellow blaze alerts you to the fork at which the route to Puffer Pond (section 71) begins. Continue south on the side of the hill with the road pulling away from the marshes along the Flow. Less than ten minutes later, after a very short descent, you reach Puffer Pond Brook. Not even a hundred yards beyond, cross the unnamed brook which drains the slopes of Puffer Mountain. It is the guide for the route described in section 74.

The continuing route, still following an obvious old roadbed, heads slightly west of south, climbing slightly. The route is through a wonderful forest of tall trees. The next 0.6-mile section is without obvious markings, making it difficult to describe the intersection with the path to Wakely Brook. You may count four intermittent stream crossings in that stretch, which takes about twenty minutes to walk. The right fork to Wakely Brook does have a couple of red marks, as does the route you are following, but do not count on them.

About 300 yards beyond the fork, the path swings to the southeast and begins a long, gentle rise. Near the top of the rise, the roadway is partly washed out by a crossing intermittent stream. Mark that spot, for within 200 yards of it, in a level stretch of the road, there is a fork to the right. You will need to find that spot if you wish to attempt the bushwhack to Humphrey Mountain Garnet Mine (section 72). It is a brisk hour-and-twenty-minute, just-over-three-mile walk to this spot.

Since someone has cleared the continuing route south, it is now the more obvious route, though it really only disappears after another half mile. Near its end, it climbs a hillside in a lovely ferny glen, which marks the best place to turn around and head back.

Both this route and the flow itself are good for ski-touring. Kings Flow is shallow and peppered with picturesque twisted stumps, especially at the southern end. The inaccessible swampy southern shore has many spruce-covered promontories to ski around in winter.

69 Puffer Pond from the Northwest

Hiking, fishing, camping, skiing
2 miles, 1¹/₄ hours, 600-foot climb, red markers

Walk east on the old road from the parking area at Kings Flow, cross a bridge as you enter the woods, and in 200 yards fork right onto a narrow, red-marked trail that clings to the side of the hill. The trail register is six or seven minutes away at the boundary of the Wilderness Area. After a gradual uphill, you begin to see wetlands off to your right. You follow them and the open water that surrounds Carroll Brook for ten minutes more, until the trail seems to split. The path right leads to a beaver dam, your causeway to cross the flooded brook. If you stay left on the trail, you find that you are forced back to the same beaver dam crossing.

Across the brook the trail turns sharply left to follow the southern edge of the flows. This chain of beaver dams, marshes, and open flows along Carroll Brook remains one of the really handsome ones—enjoy the stumps and reflections. Follow the marshes for another eight minutes or so, then head uphill, slightly south of east, along a small stream. Within ten minutes, in a very small clearing, the trail makes a right-angle turn to the south. A sign says it is 0.8 mile to Puffer Pond. (Notice, to your left, the faint beginning of a blue-marked trail; that is the start of section 70.) From this clearing, you can see the cliffs on the southeast face of Chimney Mountain.

Turning right, you head uphill, fairly steeply, following a small stream, then crossing it to reach a height-of-land in ten minutes. You climb over 400 feet from Carroll Brook. A cleft angles sharply left while the trail finds a steep way down across a rocky outcrop. In less than twenty-five minutes from the intersection, after descending nearly 200 feet from the height-of-land, you reach the lean-to at the shore of the pond. Several aluminum boats greet you. If you use them to fish or explore the pond, return them as you find them.

You may want to look for signs of an old logging camp located at the west end of the lake, near the outlet. The surrounding forests were all logged, first for pine and hemlock, later for pulpwood. No sign remains of any other cluster of buildings on the southeast corner of the pond. The trail follows the north shore of the pond east to the second lean-to, and on to Old Farm Clearing (section 86).

70   Puffer Pond via the John Pond Trail

Cross-country skiing
6.5 miles, 3¹/₂ hours, blue-marked trail

This is a popular trail with skiers who make the traverse from Old Farm Clearing, so it is described from south to north. It connects the John Pond Trail (section 62) with the Puffer Pond Trail (section 69). The 3.7-mile segment described here was built to assure state access to Puffer Pond at a time when access through Kings Flow was questionable. The trail to Puffer Pond from the John Pond parking area is very long, 6.5 miles total. Because of unplowed roads, the through trip from Thirteenth Lake using this segment is over 13 miles. The steep grades heading north from Puffer Pond to intersect this trail require a very strong and skilled skier. Even this portion of the through trip requires moderate skills.

Because it offers such a long trip to Puffer Pond, there is almost no hiking along it. There is obvious foot tread only in the north and in a few scattered places. From the looks of the spoor you will swear that the tread was worn by bears, not other hikers.

At the small clearing on the Puffer Pond Trail, head north, descending gently to a very wet, marshy area. You soon cross a fairly good-sized stream, a tributary of Carroll Brook, and continue downhill to rock-hop across a second tributary in just a couple of minutes. Look left up at the ledges on Chimney—you are quite close to that mountain's steep eastern flanks. The trail rises and falls as it curves along the convoluted western flanks of Bullhead Mountain, hugging the eastern side of a draw that lies between it and Chimney Mountain.

The forest, almost all hardwoods, is mature and open, a delightful place to walk in spite of the concealed trail. The maples are tall and stately, the witch hobble not too thick beneath. As you contour around the mountain's flanks, you occasionally find yourself heading almost east, then back north again. You remain about fifty feet above the valley floor to your left, gradually descending, with many ups and downs.

After about fifty minutes, you enter a small draw and follow it down. You cross several small streams that drain from your right and reenter a majestic forest. The trail finally appears to be following an old road. An hour and a quarter from the clearing, you reach a definite fork in the roadway. Straight ahead the trail goes up along a fairly large stream that drains the northern flanks of Bullhead Mountain. The road/path to the right is obviously used by hunters to reach the wild and forbidding northeast slopes of Bullhead.

The trail makes a sharp ninety-degree turn to the left and quickly descends to the level of a spruce plantation. It heads through the plantation and out into a swamp, briefly, then makes a hop-a-rock crossing of the stream. It could be a wet crossing in high water. This point is two minutes, through another plantation, from the John Pond Road, fifteen minutes from the pond, and fifty minutes or less from the parking area.

71   Puffer Pond from the West
Path, old road

At the turn of the century a road followed the east side of Kings Flow and then curved east to follow the outlet of Puffer Pond to the pond itself. The road served the logging operations centered around the pond. The USGS map for 1898, reissued in 1923, noted them with a legend that signified "private or poor road." Nevertheless, the road served for a time as a part of the principal route from Indian Lake to North Creek.

A path, informally marked with red disks, follows the old roadway. Walk south along the east side of Kings Flow to the intersection 0.8 mile beyond Carroll Brook, as described in section 68. When the old roadway leaves the level route beside Kings Flow, it makes a long, gentle traverse of the shoulder of a small hill, curving gradually to the east and intersecting the Puffer Pond outlet at a point about 120 feet above the flow. For the rest of the climb to Puffer Pond, the road parallels the outlet on the north side, staying quite close to it except in the last 200 yards. Here it climbs to high ground north of the outlet. A search along the outlet near the pond may turn up signs of the old logging camp, which was last used about 1918.

If you have never tried to follow an old road that has become overgrown

Humphrey Mountain's heart-shaped crest rises above Kings Flow

through disuse, this would be a good first attempt. Since the roadway parallels the outlet, you could not get lost. Fishermen have recently used it, and informal blazes of red and bottle tops mark the route. There is an obvious footpath, but it has new growth of witch hobble and ferns. Some of this, plus the blowdowns, is being removed by those who use the route for cross-country skiing. While you can easily follow the road, it does contain all the problems you might meet in attempting to walk along one of the area's really overgrown old roads.

It is nearly a 3-mile walk from the Kings Flow camp to Puffer via this route, nearly 1 mile longer than the arc to the north below Chimney Mountain (section 69). The climb is a little more gradual and the walk beside Puffer Pond outlet is certainly lovely. The stream has several pretty pools and small ledges and falls. Combine this walk with the one described in section 69 to make a loop hike. The loop requires less than three and a half hours of walking, so on a day excursion there is plenty of time left for fishing at Puffer Pond.

Since the roadway has been cleared, the gentle climb offers the best ski-touring route for the through trip from Kings Flow to Thirteenth Lake. It remains a long and strenuous trip, however, and the trip east from Puffer Pond has several steep sections (see section 86), so it should be used only by skiers with at least intermediate skill. If there is new snow or if others have not skied the trail, it will be necessary to break trail until you get to Old Farm Clearing. This will increase the level of exertion considerably.

72 Humphrey Mountain Garnet Mine

Bushwhack, campsites, mine exploration

A small open-pit garnet mine is located on the north face of Humphrey Mountain at about the 2500-foot level. The mine site was owned by Howard Kenyon before it was purchased by the state for taxes. According to Shirley Hall Matzke, her father, Cleon Hall, worked for Frank Hooper at the garnet mine near Thirteenth Lake. Hooper knew there was garnet on Humphrey Mountain but did not know how rich the vein was, so he asked Hall to find out. In order not to reveal their explorations to the owner, Hall waited for threatening weather, then rode his horse, Kit, from Thirteenth Lake to the mountain via the Puffer Pond trail. He would camp near where the garnet mine was located and only blast the vein when there was thunder around. He found the vein was rich in garnet, but soon afterwards Hooper sold out to Barton and never bought the property. Even though the work there was mostly exploratory, there is a large tailings pile below the mine.

All the garnet recovered was hand-picked from the blasted rocks and even today you can see garnets in the black hornblend that makes up part of the face of a small cliff, which is all that is left of the mine site.

Read section 68 to find the place to leave the path along the east shore of Kings Flow for the Garnet Mine bushwhack. Since no clearing has been done in this area in recent years, the route which once followed old trails and blazed routes is impossible to follow. Now, it must even be considered a difficult bushwhack.

From the Kings Flow path, a route with double blazes angles downhill and disappears as it approaches the level of Humphrey Brook. You have to push through spruce and alders to reach the flow beside the brook, but a prominent glacial erratic will be a good marker for your route through the meadow. Cross the stream about 150 feet downstream from the erratic. (In trying to find a continuing roadway, we walked downstream about 200 yards and found the remains of an old dam which created this flow.)

Pick a compass course of just south of west, about 240 degrees. It is a dense forest with little ups and downs. In half a mile, you reach a series of beaver meadows, one in particular with a dense stand of newly killed spruce. There is a place to cross the flow below one of the beaver dams. Use this point to sight along Humphrey's summits to help you plan your continuing route. From here you have a good view of Humphrey's heart-shaped summit and the steep ridges below them. Look to the northwest.

You should make out a small valley below the summits and a small rise north of it. That valley is your destination.

Beyond the beaver meadows, head southwest. Within five minutes you begin to climb, and the route will get increasingly steep. You will be circling around the mountain, spiraling up it, climbing where you can. The going is rough. It is steep enough so that you have occasional glimpses through the trees—this would be a great route when the leaves are off! At times you can see Puffer's summit, at others you are looking up the flow to the cliffs on the small hill beyond the former scout camp. You may even catch sight of Chimney Mountain. There are numerous small ledges, a lot of dead-falls, and a couple of places where you will be certain you see a blazed pathway. It is just not possible to follow it for any distance.

After a rugged hour of climbing—you can now appreciate the steepness of Humphrey's cone shape—begin to look sharply. At a point where you would have to be heading almost due south to continue climbing, you should spot a small mound of rocks—the tailings pile blasted from the mine. Continue directly uphill for a hundred yards to a small ledge. This is the mine. All about you are rocks of hornblend, some with garnets still in them.

Remains of dam on Humphrey Brook

It takes about an hour to descend to the beaver flows, a half hour to return to Humphrey Brook. It is a rugged 3-mile bushwhack round trip from the Kings Flow path, even if you do not have to wander about to find your way or the mine. The bushwhack with lunch and a bit of exploring at the mine takes about three and a half hours. You should allow about seven hours for the whole trip. Add the rugged climb to the difficulty of navigating, and the trip to the mine will give you a triumphant sense of accomplishment.

73 Kings Flow Circuit
Path, ski-touring

A circuit of Kings Flow, using old roads, is still possible, though you will have to search about for the route at times. In summer, it can only be done if you reach the eastern bay of Round Pond by the route described in section 64 because you cannot cross Kings Flow dam or use boats on it.

In winter, skiers use the flow to reach a path which heads southwest from a rock about 0.2 mile south of the outlet. That path quickly intersects an old road through a lovely forest and, after a mile and a quarter—a gentle 180-foot climb—reaches that eastern bay. From here, the route is almost due south, into a notch on the small unnamed hill. The 300-foot descent from the hill is sufficiently steep on a narrowly cut route that the whole route must be rated for experts. It is 1.5 miles from Round Pond to Wakely Brook.

The section of the route that is the hardest to follow is the three-quarters mile from Wakely Brook, through open places, over Humphrey Brook, to intersect the Kings Flow path. There is a variety of blazes, paint daubs, and bottle caps which sparsely mark the route.

74 Puffer Mountain Cliffs
Most difficult bushwhack, great views

The Puffer Mountain cliffs present the greatest challenge of any bushwhack described in this guide. They should be attempted only by small groups with at least two guides who are familiar with the intricacies of bushwhacking. The 4-mile round-trip bushwhack, climbing 1700 feet, in addition to nearly 4 miles walking on a path, make this trip arduous as well

View of Gore Mountain from Humphrey Mountain Cliffs

as challenging. Instead of a route description, the following is a narrative of our trip, and it leaves much room for improvisation.

We started at the camp at Kings Flow, early enough to allow eight hours walking. We followed the path along the east shore of Kings Flow (section 68) to the outlet of Puffer Pond, a distance of 1.8 miles. The fact that we walked (ran) that stretch in forty minutes attests to our apprehension about the mountain ahead.

There is a campsite near the intersection of the trail and Puffer Pond outlet. Starting here, we crossed the outlet and followed the path for 200 yards to a small unnamed stream that flows from a valley whose head is less than 0.5 mile from the summit of Puffer. We chose this stream as the best guide to the summit area. It was not only a good route, it was an exciting and unusual one.

The stream flows from a rugged, rock-filled gorge. We walked first on the south bank, and then crossed to the north as the walking became rough. Finally the tumble of rocks and tangle of spruce drove us to the ridge north of the stream. After a 0.5-mile trek, the stream splits. We crossed to follow the south branch. There is such a jumble where the stream splits that if you do not notice the amount of water flow carefully, you might go north on the smaller stream, which is not even shown on the USGS maps.

As the stream angles southeast, a huge draw develops around it. Forty-foot cliffs rise on the south, and the ravine on the north is filled with huge spruce, hemlock, and yellow birch. We had been bushwhacking for at least an hour and fifteen minutes when we reached the head of the draw. We had climbed to the 2400-foot level, 700 feet above Kings Flow. Here the stream levels off, and the walking becomes much easier, as the cover is a high, handsome, open forest.

Then the stream does a remarkable thing; it flows from a series of smooth rock slides, most so gentle they are as easy to walk as a sidewalk in the woods. Even though it is occasionally slippery, it is a marvelous route to speed through the spruce thickets. It only requires forty-five more minutes to reach the 3000-foot level.

At this point we left the brook and headed due east. Many small ledges surround the summit area, and the walking (climbing) is fairly difficult. The forest is almost entirely spruce interspersed with a few birch; but, mercifully, the spruce are fairly large and their lower branches gone, so the walk here is unusually easy.

We continued east across the long narrow shoulder of Puffer. After three and a half hours of walking we caught sight of blue patches in the spruce, which foretold of cliff tops. We knew from studying these cliffs from other mountains, Gore and Eleventh for instance, that they were below the summit. However, distant views never told us that the spruce cover from the ridgeline down to the tops of the cliffs was almost impenetrable, nor that we would have to descend several small cliffs just to reach open cliff tops, nor that there were no level places on the tops of the cliffs on which to stand and enjoy the view! We considered ourselves very lucky to find one very small vantage spot. After enjoying it, we poked about for other openings with no success, even though the cliffs range for 0.5 mile across the eastern face of the mountain. From the vantage we could see an open cliff below and to the south, but it was impossible to find a safe, open point on the top. Heading along the cliff top to the north was even worse; we never got through the spruce that grew along the nearly vertical mountainside above the exposed vantage.

It really did not matter, for the one vantage we found was on the top of a 500-foot partially wooded cliff. You can imagine the exhilaration we felt on reaching it. I felt I was perched on top of the world, even if my perch seemed too precarious.

The view is spectacular. Beyond Bullhead and Peaked mountains on the north lies the Boreas Valley with some of the High Peaks ranging above; east of the Gothics the distinctive slide on Giant is clearly visible. Nearer views are just as great; Twin Ponds seem so close in the valley below. Past the ponds stretches the valley of Thirteenth Lake with the old Hooper Mine clearly visible as a bright red pocket in the hillside.

The cliff top is only a little lower than the summit of Gore, which seems deceptively close across the valley. With field glasses we studied the building and the huge slash of the Barton Mine 7.5 miles away. Most exciting is the range of hills that lie across the broad sweep of the valley of the East Branch: Height of Land and Eleventh mountains. Black Mountain and the Blue Hills complete the panorama on the near south. But best of all, the weather that day was so good we could see mountains to the southeast, the most obvious being Crane Mountain and Mount Blue.

We ranged south along the summit ridge looking for openings. The highest cliffs are to the south on the wooded escarpment of Puffer's eastern face: their summits are at least 100 feet below the ridge. We traveled far enough north on the ridge to learn we were wise not to ascend via our second-choice route. The long, gentle shoulder from the Twin Ponds side on the northeast and the Thirteenth Lake to Puffer Pond Trail would have ended in a miserable climb through small, dense spruce below the summit ridge.

We circled north and west around the summit intending to descend to the north almost to the outlet of Puffer Pond, then to swing toward the west through the logically less steep draw. At first it was difficult to find places to descend around the ledges that surround the summit area. The problem was compounded because we tried to find the exposed ledges that are visible from Puffer Pond. Two hundred vertical feet below the summit ridge, the forest opens out. Birch and hardwoods predominate, but ledges are everywhere, many too high for hiking. We could see Puffer Pond at several points and could often gauge our progress by the prominent cliff on Bullhead Mountain. As soon as we had descended about 400 feet we found ourselves in a gentler valley. The surprise of the day was discovering what must have been a logging road angling across the north face. We were amazed at the steepness of the road, which was last used over sixty years ago. It was so faint it might be difficult to find again, but it certainly aided our descent. It seemed to disappear as we approached the valley of Puffer Pond Brook, so we headed straight down to the brook and crossed it to the path, which we intersected just below the 2100-foot level.

While the route up the unnamed creek was fairly difficult, I would repeat the trip using the same loop. At least the stream directs you to a point due west of the best vantage. I know I will go back, perhaps wearing armor plate, and search again for more outlooks along the cliff tops.

From Indian Lake Village East

INDIAN LAKE VILLAGE is the place to restock supplies, find lodging, and obtain current information about the woods. Many of the walks in the guide are within an hour's drive of the village. Most of the land along the south side of NY 28 east of the village toward North River and Thirteenth Lake is private. Only two locations, a private cross-country ski area and a small pond, are accessible from the highway (section 75 and 76).

75 Abanakee Loop
Cross-country skiing

The Abanakee Loop is a well-designed cross-country ski area, 0.5 mile east of Indian Lake village on NY 28. The loop has 4.5 miles of trail on state land plus 1.5 miles on private lands.

The system was laid out south and east of Geandreau's Cabins; public access is from a parking area behind the motel. Ski southeast of the parking area and cross a brook on a bridge to reach the marked loops. The trails are not laid out on level ground; rather they are designed to acquaint cross-country skiers with mountain and forest wilderness conditions. The loop is a transition for novice-to-intermediate skiers between level beginner trails and the varied terrain encountered on wilderness treks. A map of the loop and additional information are available at the motel office.

76 Prier Pond
Path, picnic site, bog

The path to Prier Pond brings you in an easy fifteen-minute walk to a typical small Adirondack pond. Most of the shoreline is marshy and there are a few bog plants, which indicate that this pond is dying. Pines at its northeastern end mark the only high ground around the pond, with spruce, alder, birch, and maple surrounding the rest of the shoreline.

If you are leaving North River going toward Indian Lake about lunch-time there is an attractive picnic site at the shallow pond to the south of NY 28. Going west you turn left on a paved road just 4.4 miles from Thirteenth Lake Road in North River (1.5 miles from Cleveland Road). Go past the old Dew Drop Inn with the porch on two sides and park on the right across from a large old apple tree.

Up the hill to the right of the apple tree, walk south through an open area. Past some junk at the end of the opening, the path bears left down the hill. You can follow old blazes on the trees which were made by hunters some time ago. After about a ten-minute walk along the blazed path, cut downhill through the woods, roughly going east of south. There is no path, but in about 200 yards you will see the pond. Look for an opening in the trees and go out on the shore, which is boggy.

Prier Pond was named after a family of early settlers, the Daniel Priers. During the late 1800s an inn at the height-of-land near the Prier farm served summer visitors, who were carried by stagecoach from the end of the rail line at North Creek to the resorts at Blue Mountain Lake. The old stagecoach road, Ordway Road, may still be found where it crosses the Prier farm.

The shore is marshy, but you can explore the inlet, which is full of sphagnum moss and typical bog plants. A short bushwhack around the pond's north end brings you to the high ground near the outlet. Beaver often settle in the outlet of the pond, and ducks find it a good nesting place. Look for signs of muskrat.

The pond is ringed by large pine, and lily pads dot the surface around the edges. Generally you will frighten ducks, which will wheel overhead. There is a view of Davis Mountain across the pond and Casey rises on the left (north). To the south, tall tamarack line the shore, showing a rich golden color in the fall. The south end has a sphagnum mat with many pitcher plants, sundew, and horned bladderwort. Sweet gale lines the shore, so prepare for wet feet if you wish to explore the plants. Enjoy lunch by this easily accessible quiet place.

There is a second path to Prier Pond that leads from Dew Drop Camp to the height-of-land by the pines. It is a bit easier to follow, but since it crosses private land, you should have permission from someone at the camp in order to use it.

The Garnet Hills

IN 1878, HENRY Barton, who was in the abrasives business in Philadelphia, was informed of the discovery of garnet deposits on Gore Mountain. He quickly leased the land and started a successful business mining and marketing garnets as abrasives. Erwin Miller of North River has researched the history of garnet mining in the Adirondacks from 1878 to the present. He has not only shared his findings with me, but has helped explore the mountains where pockets of garnets can be found.

Garnets, the ruby-colored crystals that appear on almost every mountain in the northeastern half of the area described in this guide, shaped the economy of North Creek and reshaped the profiles of several mountains.

The twelve-sided crystal is most prevalent around the 2400-foot level. Look for it on your walks over the mountains described in this chapter. Garnets from several mines were occasionally used for jewels, but their principal use has been in industry. North Creek garnets are renowned for their hardness and the way they fracture with a sharp cutting edge. Their excellent abrasive qualities make them especially desirable for the woodworking industry.

In the 1880s, when production of garnets began, the only method of separating them from the ore was to break them loose with a small hand pick. The find on Gore Mountain contained pockets of large crystals, some the size of a bushel basket. At first, hand drills were used to place charges of black powder, which broke up the rock ledges and exposed the crystals. Sledges and then little picking hammers were employed to finish freeing the garnet. In winter, heavy horse-drawn sleds carrying the mineral were pulled from the mine on Gore Mountain to the railroad at North Creek. This primitive method was used at the Barton mine until 1926.

In 1893, Frank Hooper, a mining engineer, devised a scheme for mechanically separating the garnet from ore, based on a newly patented vanning jug that required quantities of water. The process made use of the high specific gravity of garnet, so the surrounding rock was swirled away while the heavier mineral was recovered from the bottom of huge separating tanks. His method was crude, but it still enabled him to harvest 95 percent of the garnet from his mines.

Frank Hooper's first mine was on the northeast side of Ruby Mountain. By the summer of 1894 he had constructed both a mill for separating the ore and homes for his workers, all from lumber planed at a sawmill he built nearby. By 1908, he had transferred his North River Garnet Company mill to a new mine on Thirteenth Lake, where the remains of his operation can be seen today (section 80). He laid out roads and built a whole town, some of whose buildings survive as Garnet Hill Lodge on the hill above Thirteenth Lake. Over one hundred men were employed in twelve-hour shifts, each man earning two dollars a day, or less. The forty-five buildings he constructed for his workers included a school, a blacksmith shop, and a boarding house for seventy-five men where the cook, Zora Brown, prepared forty loaves of bread, thirty-five pies, and a washtub of beef six days a week for the five meals a day consumed by the two shifts of mill workers.

When the supply of ore on Thirteenth Lake ran out in 1928, Hooper did not move his mine to a new site on Ruby Mountain. Instead, he sold his business and his new Ruby Mountain find to the Barton Mine Corporation, which for fifty years supplied 90 percent of the world's garnets for abrasives from its Gore Mountain mine. In 1984, the company completed construction of a new mill on the south side of Ruby Mountain and closed the Gore Mountain operations.

A mineral shop is open at the old Gore Mine in the summer from June until September and a guide will take groups through the abandoned mine for a small fee. The mineral shop is reached by taking the Barton Mines Road off NY 28 near the North River General Store. The new mine site, processing buildings, and tailing piles have been carefully located (in consultation with the Adirondack Park Agency) so that the visual impact of the operations is negligible. Barton continues to be a major world supplier of garnets for technical industrial abrasives. The mine is the largest employer in the area, although recreational use of these lakes and hills by cross-country skiers, hikers, and campers is increasing.

Pockets of garnet can be found on many wilderness walks. As you explore the regions covered in sections 77 through 84, look for the black pockets of hornblend that surround the dark red crystals. These garnets were formed about a billion years ago, when the Adirondacks were newly formed sedimentary deposits intruded by three igneous rocks: anorthosite, gabbro, and syenite. Each of the intrusive rocks was subjected to severe pressures and temperatures. The effect on the gabbro was to permit pockets of the elements that constitute the garnet to collect. Slow cooling allowed the growth of the huge crystals deep within the earth. Erosion and glaciers later carried away the overlying rock, exposing the igneous rocks and their mineral pockets as we see them today.

77 Ruby Mountain

Difficult bushwhack, magnificent views

The summit of Ruby Mountain is state land, but all approaches to the mountain from adjacent roads cross private land, so access is complicated. It is definitely desirable to seek permission to cross that private land, as the views from the bare rock that edge the summit are magnificent.

The summit is a rough triangle with an apex to the south. From outlooks near the south, Peaked and Slide mountains are visible and the splendid range of mountains that rim the East Branch of the Sacandaga River can be seen in the distance beyond Thirteenth Lake. In this range, Black Mountain and the Blue Hills are easy to distinguish.

If you study Ruby's eastern ridge from NY 28 east of North River you will notice the configuration of cliffs and outlooks ranging across the mountain. There are open rock patches along the entire southeast side of the triangular summit. Gore Mountain is visible to the southeast from these ledges, with Height of Land Mountain south of it and Balm of Gilead in the middle ground behind Thirteenth Lake.

Most of the eastern exposures look directly down the Hudson River valley, with Moxham Mountain to the north. The rock ledges on the northern end of the ridge seem to hang above the open pit of the abandoned garnet mine Frank Hooper opened in 1894. The pit, which is nestled at the eastern foot of the mountain, was the site of the Adirondack's first garnet mill.

All of the land south of the summit benchmark is presently owned by the Barton Mines, which has moved all their mining operations to Ruby Mountain. Here, garnet deposits are estimated to be as large as Gore, but are more difficult to extract. The crude assays made by Frank Hooper and his chief engineer, H. Vogel, in the early nineteenth century were remarkably accurate. This land is posted and dangerous to cross because of the blasting that accompanies the mining operation.

To gain access across the private land, write to Robert Davidge, Box 337, Red Hook, NY 12571, and include a self-addressed postcard. State approximately when you want to walk the mountain and how many will be in your group. Remember, accesses to the mountain and the ledges across the summit are as free of litter and as clean as the birches that dazzle the hillside. Please keep it that way, so others may continue to obtain permission to cross the private land.

Drive 0.7 mile southwest on Cleveland Road from NY 28 to a right turn onto a logging road on Mr. Davidge's property, which is currently being logged. The climb uses the logging road for the first part of the hike to shorten the bushwhack. The road takes you almost to Aldous Brook and the old dam behind which Frank Hooper stored water for his garnet mill in the early 1900s.

From Cleveland Road, walk uphill 150 yards to a small pond and continue west, uphill, to a cleared area. Still following the principal logging route, head downhill, as the road swings to the south around a small hill, across a draw in a cleared area, and uphill, southwest. The road curves west around a second hill and heads downhill, and reaches a fork where you stay straight (left leads back to Cleveland Road). Your route ends in 200 yards in a small clearing and the pond is just 100 yards downhill.

The view up the pond is to Little Davis Mountain. Note the beautiful handcut stones in the dam, where it is easiest to cross the brook.

Aldous Pond

Now bushwhack west along the south side of the pond and look for a huge old beaver house on the way. When you approach the end of the pond, turn to a compass course of 220 degrees magnetic. This takes you on a steep climb directly up the mountain through open, second-growth timber with a scattering of birch. The number of small ledges increases as you reach the ridge below the summit. Depending on the accuracy of your compass course, you will intercept a yellow-marked state line near the ridge. Proceed up this marked line, approximately 250 degrees magnetic. The property line comes to a cliff outlook. Better views from open cliffs can be found just below the line.

The entire northeastern side of the mountain is easy to walk. White birch and the marginal shield fern, *Dryopteris marginalis*, crown the rock ledges and an occasional lady's tresses orchid graces the boulder-strewn lower slopes. Rusty woodsia ferns thrive on the dry edges of the bare rocks.

Walk along the ridge to find more vantage points. All of the land below the cliffs to the southeast is private. This route should enable you to stay on state land all the way to the summit after leaving Aldous Brook.

The bushwhack involves an 800-foot climb and more than three miles of walking for the round trip, which can take as much as four hours. Allow plenty of time to enjoy the summit ridge and to follow navigational directions carefully.

78 Thirteenth Lake

Canoeing, fishing, camping, swimming

The principal accesses to the Garnet Hills are from Thirteenth Lake, which was formed in a fault valley and is bordered on the northwest by precipitous hills. The shores of the two-mile-long lake are state owned, with the exception of a very small section on the east. Access to the lake is by way of Thirteenth Lake Road, which leaves NY 28, 0.5 mile west of North River. It heads west and south, beside Thirteenth Brook, through Christian Hill, and forks 3.5 miles from NY 28. The left, east, road goes to Old Farm Clearing and Garnet Hill Lodge, and the west road leads to a parking lot located about 200 yards from Thirteenth Lake. There is a barrier to motorized vehicles at the parking lot since this is a boundary line of the Siamese Ponds Wilderness Area. Small boats and canoes can be carried (or small trailers with boats pushed) around the barrier and along the graveled path to the lake.

This site can be used to put in a small boat for fishing, camping, or sailing. The lake is stocked with brook trout and landlocked salmon. Special fishing regulations apply at Thirteenth Lake, which means trout must be at least twelve inches long to keep (with a limit of three fish per day) and landlocked salmon must be eighteen inches long (limit of one per day). Most important, only artificial lures may be used.

There are six campsites at the north end of the lake, which can be reached on foot, and several along the steep western shore, most easily reached by canoe. The best sites are on the east shore and are also reached by canoe. There is no charge for camping on Thirteenth Lake. Permits given by the local Department of Environmental Conservation Forest Ranger are required for camping on the lakeshore if your stay exceeds three nights. There is excellent swimming in the lake from the sand beach on the north end and off the rocks; some leeches are found along shores with muddy bottoms.

Thirteenth Lake is also the starting point for the trips described in the remaining sections of this guide, 79 through 90. A footpath along the west shore leads from the launching site south to Peaked Mountain Brook. The path that traverses rocky ledges above the lake offers lovely vistas of the lake and the surrounding mountains.

Adventurous hikers can also start from the launching site to improvise a scramble up either Little Thirteenth or Big Thirteenth mountains, which are to the west. Both mountains have a series of ledges and cliffs from which there are good views of the lake, beyond which rises Gore Mountain to the east.

79 Garnet Hill Lodge

Cross-country skiing

In the past three years, an extensive network of ski trails has been developed around Garnet Hill Lodge, which sits high above Thirteenth Lake, and at High Winds, which occupies buildings at the abandoned Barton garnet mine site on Gore Mountain. Both offer overnight accommodations. There is a fee for skiing the trails on private land, and both places offer return bus rides for skiers who wind down from the slopes of Pete Gay or Harvey Mountains. Some of these ski trails are quite beautiful—and challenging. Maps are available at the lodges. You can see the High Peaks from the switchbacks on the Joe Pete Trail on Harvey. The

Garnet Hill Lodge Trail that meanders down to Rogers Road on a series of old roads is a delightful and gentle deep woods route.

The road to Garnet Hill Lodge is a marked left turn from Thirteenth Lake Road; the road to High Winds heads directly up the mountain from North River. In addition to the trails on private land, the resorts groom (pack by skiing) trails on Thirteenth Lake, along the road to Old Farm Clearing (next chapter), and across the Vly at the headwaters of Halfway Brook (section 82). Garnet Hill Lodge leads groups to Puffer Pond (section 86), to the East Branch of the Sacandaga (sections 85 and 89), and to Buck Meadow Flow (section 90).

The region's easiest ski trail is a circuit that combines the road to the lodge's private beach, a trek down frozen Thirteenth Lake, and the path from Elizabeth Point on the lake to the Old Farm Clearing Road. The views along the lake are unsurpassed in the southern Adirondacks. Birch-lined shores on the east and steep, cliff-faced mountains on the west frame the lake.

80 The Hooper Mine and Putty Pond

Short, easy path

A slash of brilliant red rock edges a semicircular scar near the crest of the small hill east of Thirteenth Lake. The walls of the cut mark the abandoned Hooper garnet mine. The mine is on state land, but access is over private lands owned by the Garnet Hill Lodge (section 79). Permission to cross them will be granted to those who wish to walk to the mine, but check in at the lodge.

The path begins at the cross-country ski-touring center run by Garnet Hill Lodge. The road to the center is well marked; if you are up at the Lodge, drive down the hill and take the first turn to the left. The path to the mine begins across from the ski-touring center to the left of the tennis court. One hundred yards up the hill the road forks. The left fork leads to a private home. The right fork, which is marked, winds on up the hill to the old open-pit mine.

Walk across the floor of the mine to the northwest corner to discover the remains of Hooper's mill. His system for separating ore involved the use of much water and depended on gravity to do the work. As ore moved down the hill, it was crushed, separated, and dried. The huge tailings pit is below and to the north.

One hundred feet before the road enters the mine a narrow footpath winds around a small hill to the east rim of the pit. From here there are lovely views of Thirteenth Lake and the mountains beyond. If you seek a vantage nearer the north rim, you will find views southwest beyond the lake to the cliffs of Puffer Mountain. If you look northwest toward Ruby Mountain you will see some large buildings on the slopes of Ruby at about the same elevation. This is the new Barton Mine plant which is now processing ore on that mountain.

The Putty Pond, which was a settling pond for the Hooper Mine mill water, is reached by going down a road to the right of the tennis courts. About 100 yards down the road there is a sign indicating the Putty Pond and Wilderness Trail, which bears off to the right. The pond is now dry, but is full of marvelous bog plants, including the frog orchid, *Habenaria viridis.*

81 William Blake Pond and the Balm of Gilead

Trail, cross-country skiing, bushwhack

There is a trail up the hill to the southeast of the Garnet Hill ski-touring center, leading to a once dammed pond that was one of the sources of water for Frank Hooper's mill. A faint path leads off of this trail to the south to a magnificent cliff on the Balm of Gilead. By bushwhacking you can combine these two paths into a lovely short walk. In winter the trail to William Blake Pond is popular with cross-country skiers with intermediate ability. The beginning of the paths cross private land so ask at the lodge or the ski-touring center for permission.

The trail begins to the left of the tennis court across from the ski-touring center just as if you were going up to the old Hooper mine (section 80). Go up the hill 100 yards to where the right fork leads to the mine. At this point a path bears right marked "Overlook Trail" and a sign labeled "William Blake Pond" is planned. This path winds south on the contour for several minutes' walk until you see a large house to the right. At this point you are on state land and the trail goes to the left up the hill. The trail is cleared and visible. It once followed large pipes from the pond down to the mill operations. The pipes are gone now except for a short distance below the pond.

Map VII Sections 76-87 and 89-90

Based on USGS 15' Thirteenth Lake
and Newcomb Quadrangles

Path
Trail
Bushwhack
Road
Cliffs

0   1 mile

N

Halfway up the hill the trail intercepts and follows the outlet stream. Stay on the trail and it will lead you to the former pond, named Wm. Blake Pond on old maps. Someone has trapped the beaver out so there is little water in it now. You can see the manmade dam with large hand-hewn square rocks at the outlet. Dead trees rise starkly from the level area now filled in with high tufted grass. Beaver move in and out of the area so in the future beaver may return and be observed at work before dusk and early in the morning.

From the outlet, head southwest to a ridge 2300 feet above sea level that traverses the northernmost of the three knobs that constitute the summit of the Balm of Gilead. A route more toward west would be the most direct route, but if you head southwest to the ridge and then walk northwest along it, looking for the cliff, that is your destination. You will pass a stand of the largest white birch that I have ever found in the wilds. There are several rocky promontories, and you will have no trouble finding the one with the best outlook; it has a view southwest toward Puffer Mountain. On the west you should recognize Bullhead, Slide, and Peaked mountains, with the slides on Blue Mountain visible to the left of Peaked. Almost the entire length of Thirteenth Lake and the mountain range west of the lake will be spread out below you.

The hill was named for a sterile variety of the Balsam Poplar, the Balm of Gilead tree. The ends of its branches are gummy and give off a spicy fragrance in spring. In the nineteenth century, pungent odor from the trees on the Balm of Gilead was noticed as far away as Christian Hill, thus inspiring the mountain's name.

The walk to the pond and the bushwhack to the cliff should take about one and a half hours. The total distance is under 2 miles.

Northeast of, or behind, the cliff, there is an informal path with some old and new blazes. It winds a little west of north down the mountain and is generally hard to follow. It is scheduled to be marked in the near future, so, again, check at the lodge if you wish to follow it.

The path comes down the hill near the Putty Pond dam, the old settling pond for the water used to separate garnets from the rock tailings (section 80). Complete your short walk by crossing the Putty Pond area to a road and following it back. The pond is now an open grassy area, with some sphagnum and bog plants, an excellent place to study a wide variety of flora.

The return from the hill by the faint path through the Putty Pond is about 0.5 mile long and requires about a half hour.

82   Halfway Brook to Thirteenth Lake Road

Cross-country skiing, bushwhack

A route that combines cross-country skiing with a bushwhack may seem odd, but the middle section of this trip is hard to follow in the summer. The route follows logging roads and an old trail from Barton Mines Road, where it crosses Halfway Brook, northwest towards Thirteenth Lake. The 2-mile middle section from the vly to William Blake Pond is overgrown but is marked occasionally with blue paint. Going uphill, it zigzags back and forth through witch hobble and striped maple. The blue paint marks applied in winter are seven feet above the ground, and are often obscured by leaves. A compass is recommended in case you lose your bearings. (Trail markings may be improved in the near future.) In winter it is easier to follow and with good snow it is a pleasant 3-mile trail for intermediate cross-country skiers.

The entrance to the trail at Halfway Brook is reached by the Barton Mines Road, which leaves NY 28 near the North River General Store. You drive up the mountain 3.9 miles to a slight depression where the brook flows through a culvert under the road. There is no parking space and your car must be left on the side of the road as far off as possible. The entrance to the trail is a cleared path on the right, which passes over an interesting old culvert.

It is about 0.3 mile down an attractive, balsam-lined, old logging road to the vly. In summer, sections of the path are wet and require slight detours or rock hopping. After a short walk you reach a large beaver dam that has backed water over the path. After ten minutes you cross the small brook and shortly thereafter you will see the vly through the trees to the left of the trail. In the summer the entire surface of the vly is dotted with yellow bull-head lily. If you approach the water quietly through the evergreens you may see a great blue heron standing motionless in the shallows.

In winter you can leave the trail temporarily and ski out on the vly. There is a large beaver house in the middle to explore. Gore Mountain, with the precipitous walls of the garnet mine pits, looms above you to the south. A fire tower and two radio antennas identify its summit, which is spectacular when covered with early morning hoar frost.

The trail does not go to the water's edge, but crosses twenty feet from it in a small depression and bears uphill to the right. Look carefully for the blue paint marks as there is little discernible trail through the hobble bush.

In about fifty feet there is a blue arrow on a tree pointing right and the path makes an angle turn. It later zigzags back and forth up the hill and is difficult to follow in the summer as leaves often hide the paint marks. (It is also hard to backtrack, since the blazes are only from east to west). In winter the trail is frequently skied and tracks will generally be visible. After about a 0.5-mile climb the trail levels off and parallels a steep rocky ridge on the north.

After a while you descend gradually and eventually arrive at the top of a long, steep slope. In fast snow it is hard for even experienced skiers to hold a snowplow and there is no run-out at the end. Beginner to moderate skiers should sidestep down the upper portions of this slope. Thereafter the trail descends gradually to the upper portion of William Blake Pond. In the winter you can ski out, west, over this open wetland which has an interesting landscape of dead cedar trees and large hummocks of snow-covered grass. It is a typical former beaver pond that is being filled in and reclaimed by nature. In summer it is necessary to bushwhack along the north side of the wetland and pond as the old trail has not been cleared.

The Hooper Mine

From the outlet of William Blake Pond (see section 81) it is approximately 0.5 mile down to the Garnet Hill Lodge Ski Touring Center. It is a wide, fairly gradual trail which can be handled by skiers with a reliable snowplow, although if the track is fast it is easy to build up speed. The trail leaves the Siamese Ponds Wilderness Area near a private home and you go out the dirt road beside the tennis courts to the road at the Ski Center. This is private property, so before leaving a car there you should check at the Ski Center or the Lodge (section 79).

This trail was used when the garnet mine was opened at Gore Mountain, after the Hooper Mine near Thirteenth Lake was closed in 1928. Frank Hooper (who was an outdoorsman, hunter, and fisherman) and other men from the old mine walked to work from their homes above Thirteenth Lake over the hill to the new mine. It now makes a challenging short ski tour and a pleasant summer hike if you set up a car shuttle.

83 Peaked Mountain Pond

Camping, hiking, swimming, fishing
2.25 miles one way, 1¼ hours, 550-foot climb

Peaked Mountain Pond has become a very popular fishing, hiking, and camping destination. This gem of a lake in the shadow of its own rock-covered peak is most attractive, but its short trail probably accounts for its numerous visitors. The trail is to be managed as a wilderness route, so markings are not numerous. As a result, you will find several difficult places to follow along this trail, as well as on the continuation up Peaked Mountain (section 84).

A fifteen-minute canoe trip or a mile-long walk south along the footpath on the west shore of Thirteenth Lake will put you at the Peaked Mountain Pond trailhead. For the walk along the shore, head south from the campsite that is just to the west of the canoe launching site of section 78. The trail passes several campsites and after ten minutes climbs behind a series of ledges and small cliffs. These cliffs continue for ten minutes or so, then you descend to a boat landing site in a cove. You can identify this cove from a canoe by its position below the draw, south of Little Thirteenth Mountain and by a rock slide that punctuates the end of the cliffs.

The trailhead is 200 feet to the south, past a dripping, mossy outcrop. Peaked Mountain Brook is just beyond the trail, which is marked by one,

obscure red marker. The trail heads uphill, close to the brook; its proximity to the brook makes it possible to appreciate the many small waterfalls and cascades at the beginning of the climb. On an early spring walk, the torrent rushing over the huge boulders creates a wild scene, but even summer trickles over the ledges are lovely.

The trail climbs steeply at first, then more gently, until at 0.8 mile you cross the brook by hopping rocks. Shortly beyond, you approach the first vly with views of Slide Mountain across it. The trail stays south of the first vly, and just past it a multitude of trail markers and red flags point you back across the brook and along a narrow path through the woods. This rerouting was necessitated by beaver flooding. You emerge on the north side of the second beaver meadow of the chain that fills the upland part of the valley.

Ample markers direct you around this meadow and back to the south side of the brook, where you continue on the old trail to the third vly, over which you see Peaked Mountain. Beaver have also flooded this vly, forcing hikers to make new routes farther and farther south away from it. The trail, sparsely marked, winds around huge boulders and up into the woods. This place, just short of 2 miles from lakeshore, has proved confusing on the return trip, so note well the twists and turns in the trail.

Continue through the woods beyond the third vly, out of sight of the brook. Sparse red markers point you over a ridge to the edge of the pond immediately south of its outlet, an hour and a quarter's walk from Thirteenth Lake.

Many of the existing campsites along the shore are too close to water and much degraded from overuse. These have been marked with No Camping disks, which have a way of disappearing. There is one permitted campsite about midway along the south shore and two on the peninsula that juts out into the north shore.

The same special fishing regulations that apply at Thirteenth Lake for size and use of artificial lures also apply here. You can swim from the rock ledges at the edge of the bay near the outlet and enjoy taking pictures of the white bleached stumps on the north shore. White birch stand out from the hillside above, pointing to the soft grey rock outcrops that lead to the summit of Peaked Mountain. If you walk along the beach around the pond, you will find rocks with pockets of garnets.

Peaked Mountain Pond

84 Peaked Mountain

Trail, hiking
0.8 mile, ¾ hour, 660-foot vertical rise, red flagging

A new trail has been flagged to the summit of Peaked Mountain, which rises 660 feet above its pond. The new trail was needed because many people got lost descending from the summit. The views from Peaked extend 360 degrees and are as rewarding as those from much more strenuous climbs.

To find the flagged route, hop rocks to cross the outlet of Peaked Pond, heading around the north shore on one of the several footpaths. Stay fairly close to shore until you reach the peninsula on the north shore where you will pick up the first of many flags that lead toward the summit. The flagging first points across a shallow draw at the northwest corner of the pond, where you head straight up the steep flank of the mountain in a northerly direction. The route zigzags up this first steep part, then angles right, taking a northeasterly course along the narrow ridge.

A well-worn foot tread along with the red flags identifies the new foot trail. You angle right below a small cliff and head steeply up beside it. The trail is already eroded, in places approaching the level of bedrock. After scrambling around a rock ledge and pushing through a narrow spruce- and balsam-lined passage, you emerge on an outcrop with the first view of the pond below.

The trail now angles left, away from the cliffs, and zigzags back to the tip of the tiny cone that is the summit of the mountain. There are views west to the mountains beyond Indian Lake. From the edge of the cliff you look across to Slide Mountain and back along the long chain of vlies the trail follows along Peaked Mountain Brook. Gore Mountain fills the southeast horizon, while the High Peaks are visible beyond Ruby, Davis, and Casey mountains to the north.

On the return, pay close attention to the flags and red disks along the zigzags at the beginning of the descent and also through the zigzags near the pond. Remember to follow closely around the pond until you cross the outlet, so that you can pick up the trail.

The Old Farm Clearing

OLD FARM CLEARING trailhead gives access to routes described in the remaining sections of this guide. To reach the clearing, stay straight, headed south on Thirteenth Lake Road at the point the road to Garnet Hill Lodge forks left. Drive 0.75 mile to the new parking area, which is currently being constructed near the Wilderness Area boundary. The road has been closed at this point, in accordance with the Unit Management Plan for the area. Now, you have to walk the 1.2 miles to the clearing. It takes but half an hour to do so.

South of the new parking area you pass a marked right fork to Elizabeth Point, a lovely campsite on Thirteenth Lake; shortly beyond you enter the reforestation area that fills the old clearing. The old parking area was located here with a registration booth that may be relocated back at the new parking area. Fifty feet south of the old parking area, at 1.2 miles, there is a spring. Just beyond it, the road splits to form two trails.

In 1877, Z. Van Dusen, a lumberman, lived at Old Farm Clearing. The farm, like others in the area, developed after the loggers cleared the land. Rocks pulled from his fields are scattered in piles everywhere and were even used for foundations, which are still visible.

85 East Branch Sacandaga River
Short path, cross-country skiing

Opposite the registration booth, 1.2 miles from the new parking area, a sign points east to a lovely, short, unmarked path that leads to the East Branch of the Sacandaga. It heads through rows of evergreens and past foundations to the edge of real forest, then continues generally southeast, descending gently for under a mile to end at a clearing by the river. The path is under a mile long and requires less than a half hour to walk.

In winter, the path makes a delightful, short, ski-touring route. In summer, explore the East Branch upstream from the path, where there are several lovely little waterfalls and pools. You can rock-hop up the river for 0.7 mile. The river could serve as a guide to Botheration Pond if it weren't for the huge swamp 0.3 mile before it.

Halfway Brook flows from the east into Botheration Pond through a large swamp call The Vly. The source of Halfway Brook is only 2.5 miles from the Hudson. At Botheration Pond, Halfway Brook becomes the East Branch of the Sacandaga, whose waters flow south and east to join the Hudson thirty miles south of their source.

86 Puffer Pond from the East

Trail, hiking, cross-country skiing, camping, fishing, swimming
5.5 miles one way, 3 hours, 400-foot climb

Although three routes lead to Puffer Pond from the west, only one approaches it from the east. The east trail is wide enough and sufficiently groomed to make it excellent for cross-country skiing. In places, the corduroy and rock work of the old roadbed it follows are visible. Some stream crossings on the trail have bridges; the missing ones are minor problems in summer. The high, open, mixed forest with immensely tall and straight, mature yellow birch, maple, and hemlock provides a perfect setting for a wilderness trek.

From the Old Farm Clearing registration booth in the reforestation area, 1.2 miles from the parking area, continue south on the roadway for 200 yards and then bear right on the blue-marked trail. (The continuing roadway is also blue-marked.) Walk gradually downhill through the re-forestation area, crossing several small or intermittent streams flowing to your right within the first mile. At 2.5 miles, twenty-five minutes from Old Farm Clearing, you cross a major stream that flows from Buck Meadow Flow to the south. Across the all-too-short bridge, the trail, which seems like a small rocky stream, rises and parallels Hour Pond Outlet. There is a lovely series of tiny waterfalls and a small flume on the outlet to your right—charming enough for a photograph stop.

At the top of the falls, the trail turns right to cross the outlet on a two-log bridge. You may spot the Y in the road that marks the old fork in the road. One hundred yards beyond it, a sign points the way right to the unmarked path, which intersects that roadway and leads to Hour Pond. Here, at nearly 3 miles, the Puffer Pond Trail forks left and immediately crosses the outlet, this time without a bridge.

After fording the stream, the trail begins a gradual uphill in a section so regular as to be almost dull. Nevertheless, it is a good, easy walk, and the forest cover is unusually beautiful. The trail rises gently for over 2 miles—

there are few guideposts to note—then descends a bit more steeply to reach the path to the left that leads to the first lean-to at just short of 5.5 miles.

Puffer Mountain lies to the south. If you walk south around the head of the lake from the lean-to, you can see the cliffs on Bullhead Mountain directly north of the lean-to.

There are usually boats at the pond, which is stocked with brook trout and has had a good reputation among fishermen in years past. Some of the shore is swampy, but there are a few beaches from which to swim. The trail continues west along, but set back from, the lakeshore to a second lean-to, 0.5 mile west of the first lean-to and about two-thirds of the way down the lake.

Hikers may want to make a one-way trip past the pond, using sections 69, 70, or 71 to complete the trip.

In winter, a through trip is possible for experienced skiers who have left a car at Kings Flow camp (see section 68). From the northeast lean-to proceed down the pond on the frozen surface in a southwesterly direction. At the end of the pond go into the woods a few yards from the north side of the brook and look for a trail. It will run parallel to the brook and will be marked occasionally by blazes on the trees. It is preferable to go with somebody who knows the trail unless other skiers have been through previously and you can follow their tracks.

The path has been cut out by guides who arrange hut-to-hut ski tours, but it is narrow and steep in parts. It goes southwest along the slope, roughly parallel to Puffer Pond Brook. When you can see the opening of the southern end of Kings Flow, the path cuts north. At this point you can zigzag down through the open woods to the Flow. In the mile and a quarter between the ponds you descend about 380 feet. It is about a mile down Kings Flow to the camp. The trip is tiring and strenuous and is not recommended for beginning skiers.

If you do not go on to Kings Flow when you reach Puffer Pond and return instead by way of Old Farm Clearing, you can ski the round trip in five and a half hours, but even that takes strength and stamina. On the return there are some wonderful, long ski runs, but some sections are steep. Even though the trail is relatively wide you should not attempt it unless you can hold a good snowplow and can turn in deep snow. Although the ski trail into Old Farm Clearing is maintained and tracks set by the Garnet Hill Ski Touring Center, distance is a factor which must be considered when skiing to Puffer Pond. Start early. The weather can also be very changeable and even if it is sunny when you start out, bring warm clothing for rest stops and a lunch break. You may be eating in a cold wind or a blizzard!

87   Hour Pond

Unmarked path, fishing, camping
4.4 miles, 2 hours one way, 200-foot climb

Hour Pond, which nestles between Bullhead and Hour Pond mountains, is a little over 3 miles from Old Farm Clearing. Beaver flooding has forced a rerouting of the path and made it longer than previously. Still, it is close enough for a round-trip day walk or an easy backpack trip. There are trout in the pond and the same special regulations apply to fishing here as at Thirteenth Lake.

Walk to Old Farm Clearing at 1.2 miles, west across Buck Meadow Flow outlet at 2.5 miles, and uphill for less than 0.5 mile more to the point where the Puffer Pond Trail crosses Hour Pond Outlet. Here a sign points right to the unmarked Hour Pond Path. From here it is a forty-five-minute walk to the pond, about 1.5 miles.

The path heads up and through the trees. Ahead you glimpse the cliffs on Hour Pond Mountain, which will be a dominant and inviting part of your view from the Hour Pond campsite. Follow a ridge with the outlet now far below to your left; occasionally you glimpse the broad open marshes that border the outlet. The path levels out in a draw after twenty minutes and starts down, crossing a small stream. The path, which had been heading north, curves around the head of a small draw, heading almost southwest, then angles back to descend to a campsite within sight of a large, almost dry beaver flow. All signs of the original road that the path was following are obliterated.

Walk out toward the flow and use the beaver dam to your left to cross the wet area. As a causeway it works much better than it did a few years ago! At the end, turn sharply left to follow the border of the marshes. (Yes, it does seem you are going in the wrong direction.) The narrow path heads almost south, around the side of a steep hill, curving gradually west. In a few minutes it turns away from the meadow and heads uphill through a draw. To the left of the draw is a rocky, dry stream. At the top of the draw there is a now dry beaver meadow; the dry stream was a very wet outlet when this meadow was flooded.

Beyond this meadow the path follows the outlet stream briefly, then heads uphill, only to make a sharp left turn to descend to a campsite on the shore of the pond, partway along from the outlet. At this campsite there are great views of Bullhead and Hour Pond mountains, as well as loons to keep you awake at night.

88 Twin Ponds
Path, fishing

The Twin Ponds, just to the east of Puffer Pond, have also been stocked with brook trout, and their marshy shores should discourage all but fishermen and hunters. An informal sportsmen's path to them is relatively easy to follow, once you find where it leaves the Puffer Pond Trail (section 86). People who are not familiar with the path often have to retrace their steps from Puffer Pond to find the junction. These directions may help, but you may have to retrace your steps for a short distance anyway, because the most obvious landmarks are beyond the point where the path leaves the trail as you walk from Old Farm Clearing.

Past the crossing of Hour Pond Outlet, the Puffer Pond Trail covers a long, almost level stretch in the second mile, then begins a long, gentle descent. The path to the Twin Ponds heads off to the south just before the trail begins a steeper descent into a boulder-strewn valley. You will be scarcely aware of boulders before this point, but there is an unusually large glacial erratic 100 yards beyond the junction; it makes the most obvious landmark. If you retrace your steps 100 yards west of it, you will see a tree with initials carved in it and a large arrow blaze. That marks the path whose beginning is quite concealed with new blowdowns. The path, now well marked, descends a little draw and crosses a very small stream, before turning east as it climbs a small hill. It is fairly obvious on the climb and also on the 0.5-mile descent to the first pond, even without the informal markers of red paint and red plastic squares.

While Twin Ponds' marshy shores might discourage the hiker, their history is fascinating. At the time of the "great rape of the Adirondacks," the cutting of the magnificent old pines in the nineteenth century, the lowlands of the southern shore of Twin Ponds offered a truly magnificent stand. As in a few other areas some of the pines were so large that the traditional thirteen-foot long butt, or first cut, was too heavy for man and horse. Charges of black powder were often used to split the logs in half. On the south side of the western pond lies the remains of one of the huge butts rotting, but with hard red wood inside, a lonesome testament to the forests of yesterday.

89 East Branch Sacandaga Trail South from Thirteenth Lake

Trail, camping, fishing, cross-country skiing
7.5 miles, 3 hours one way, minimal vertical rise

The state has marked the old roadway from the Old Farm Clearing south to NY 8 as a hiking trail (blue markers) and as a wilderness ski-touring trail (new pale yellow markers). The trail is one of the longest, easiest wilderness routes to walk in the Adirondacks. It is unlikely that you will meet another hiker on the 7-mile segment between the clearing and the fork toward the Siamese Ponds. Winter traveling has become so popular and this road is so perfectly suited to wilderness skiing that it is much more likely you will meet someone in winter.

This section describes the northern portion of the through route. Like the southern half of the roadway (section 18) the northern portion of the trail is a hiker's highway. But nowhere will you find a taller or more majestic forest cover overshadowing and darkening a trail; it is almost gloomy when the sun disappears behind a cloud. As you walk along, the deep quiet of the wilderness will isolate you completely from the rest of the world.

The road was once used by loggers, tanbarkers, and even early settlers, but almost all signs of civilization are lost in the woods. Only the double file of wheel ruts have survived, and they will persist for many years. Do not be fooled by the roadway, for if you walk away from it, out of sight, you are entering a true wilderness and can get lost as easily as if there were no road or trail.

The trail is long and changes little. For some hikers the only excitement will lie in the depth of the surrounding woods. From the north, leaving Old Farm Clearing, the trail quickly passes through the plantation and reforestation areas to a forest of high straight hardwoods. The birch and maple are so tall and dense that the woods has but one story, making the forest floor wide and open.

As the trail begins to drop toward the valley of the East Branch, spruce and hemlock mix with the hardwoods. You will sense the valley long before you come to it. On clear days, and especially in winter, Gore Mountain can be spotted through the trees to the east.

Hour Pond Outlet

There are a dozen split-log bridges across small streams or ravines in the 3.2 miles between Old Farm Clearing and the East Branch crossing. The hikers' bridge across the East Branch is out. In low water it is a simple matter to hop rocks across the river at the crossing, but in high water a crossing here may be almost impossible. You could camp in a small clearing near the confluence of the East Branch and Second Pond flow, less than 200 yards north of the trail crossing on the east side of the river.

The East Branch has been stocked with good-sized brook trout. A few informal fishermen's paths head toward the river from the trail.

For cross-country skiers, crossing the East Branch is the only real problem encountered in the first 4.4 miles, although the short downgrade about 1 mile south of Old Farm Clearing is steep for beginners. Fortunately, the trail is wide enough to permit skiers to control their speed by snowplowing. In winter it might be advisable, depending on conditions, for cross-country skiers to cross the river on the frozen flow above the beaver dam, upstream from the marked, but bridgeless, crossing.

As you walk along the trail on the east side of the Sacandaga, south of the crossing, you will notice that the trees are definitely shorter. Another dozen split-log bridges, some in chains through swampy areas, mark the trail segment south to Cross Brook. From the brook it is a twenty-minute walk to the open fields beside the Big Shanty flow, where there was a flood dam for logging. The clearing is full of signs of old settlements and fireplaces indicate campers have found it a good place to stop. New beaver work floods part of the flow, across which you can see the cliffs of Puffer Mountain. You walk within sight of the flow for nearly a mile.

Less than a ten-minute walk south of the clearing, at 7 miles, a newly cut trail leaves the logging road and turns west along the East Branch to the Siamese Ponds lean-to and the hiker's bridge across the river. The turn-off is unmarked, but there are blue trail markers along the new route. If you are looking for the turn, you should not miss it.

If you continue straight ahead for 0.5 mile, within fifteen minutes you will intersect the East Branch Sacandaga Trail from NY 8 (section 18). A one-day, 11.2-mile, through hike or cross-country ski trek from Thirteenth Lake to NY 8 is possible. In fact, the trail is so easy to walk that a through trek with a detour to Siamese Ponds can be made in one day. Nine and a half hours of walking will suffice for the nearly 16-mile trek. To make the detour to Siamese Ponds, take the right, unmarked fork. Bearing right, however, the next ten-minute walk along the East Branch is as pretty as any part of the trail. The river is close, the hemlock and spruce shade bunchberry-covered banks, and the trail is narrower and more fitting of a wilderness trek.

The lean-to is well placed to appreciate the river, but its view is dominated by a marvelous suspension bridge, a strange sight in the wilderness setting. From this point west to Siamese Ponds (section 19) or south to NY 8, it is unlikely that you will enjoy the feeling of remote wilderness that pervades the trek south from Old Farm Clearing.

Day hikers can easily walk these 7.5 miles in three hours, but backpackers will find four a comfortable estimate. Skiers may want to continue straight through on the logging road toward NY 8, but because the narrow section of trail leading to the bridge is level and presents no problems, they may choose to detour. Only an additional 0.2 mile permits lunch in the shelter of the lean-to.

90 Buck Meadow Flow
Difficult bushwhack, cross-country skiing

Friends have reported that there is a lovely walk along Buck Meadow, a grassy vly with occasional beaver flows. Buck Meadow is a continuation of the Thirteenth Lake drop fault, and the mountains to its west continue the sheer faces of the mountains farther north along the fault. To reach this area, follow the trail to Puffer Pond (section 86), and the path to Twin Ponds (section 88), then bushwhack around the north end of the ponds to the outlet and beside the outlet to the flow. The easiest spot to cross the flow is on the higher ground between the larger marshes to the north and south. The trek can be completed by either walking on the east side of the flow to the Puffer Pond Trail, or bushwhacking north for 0.8 mile to a small stream and then east to the East Branch Sacandaga Trail (section 89).

A logging road used to head west to the flow from what is now the East Branch Sacandaga Trail. Hunters have used it within the past fifteen years, so it is surprising that it is so difficult to find. It left the old logging road 1 mile south of Old Farm Clearing and headed just north of west. From the flow it then bore south almost to the Twin Ponds outlet, where there was a logging shack called the Tin Camp, remains of which can still be found.

Because it is so much easier to ski across Twin Ponds and the flooded marshes of Buck Meadow Flow than to bushwhack around them, it is much better to ski this circuit than to walk it.

Cliffs and Backpacking Trips

OF THE CLIFFS with views described in the guide, fourteen are reached by bushwhacks, and only five have trails or paths. There are at least nine more with no trails or paths. If you are an expert bushwhacker and if you really want to go where no one else goes, you may enjoy knowing about more cliffs with views located at the following challenging destinations:

Diamond Mountain lies northwest of Eleventh Mountain and there are many ledges on its southern face. Access is from the Siamese Ponds/East Branch Sacandaga Trail (section 18).

Bullhead Mountain has a knobby cliff on its southern face, which is north of the eastern end of Puffer Pond. Easiest access is from the height-of-land on the red trail from Kings Flow to Puffer Pond (section 69). Another range of Bullhead's cliffs hangs above Hour Pond.

Slide Mountain, between Peaked and Big Thirteenth mountains, is almost all rock on its southern and eastern sides. The whole mountain is very steep and difficult. Its views are not significantly better than those from surrounding mountains.

The peak of Corner Mountain has open patches of rock. The views are a little better than those described in the guide from the lower ledges of the mountain.

County Line Mountain, southwest of Siamese Ponds, has a few open places. They are hard to find.

There are cliffs on the little mountain east of the Robbs Creek jeep road. Closest road approach is in the vicinity of the vly, 1.8 miles from Old Route 30 (see section 32). There are good views of the Big Range from the cliffs.

Kunjamuk Mountain north of Long Pond has open rock on its southern face. Approach either from the Kunjamuk Road or from the new trail from John Mack Pond to Long Pond.

The hill between Extract and Tower brooks has cliffs facing southwest. A stiff climb up and over the hill from the Extract Brook Path should lead to their vicinity (section 4).

Every route described in the guide has been broken into segments that are day hikes. Using several parts of the guide it is possible to put together long backpacking trips. Four of those mentioned below require a car at one end and a boat at the other, or cars at both ends. Difficult bushwhacks seem to rule out all but one long loop trail with a single jumping-off point.

Thirteenth Lake to Siamese Ponds to the Siamese Ponds Trailhead beside Eleventh Mountain on NY 8: There is plenty of diversity for a week-long trip if side trips to Curtis Clearing and the cliffs on Eleventh Mountain are included.

Thirteenth Lake to Puffer Pond to Kings Flow: The trip can be extended with side trips to Hour Pond, Twin Ponds, and Chimney Mountain. Bushwhacks to Bullhead Cliffs and Puffer Mountain Cliffs are for the experts.

The Kunjamuk Road from north to south, with adequate preparations for the crossing of the Kunjamuk south of Petes Hill: This is a long day-walk or a multi-day backpack, especially if you add the trek to Long Pond Cliffs.

Indian Lake to John Mack Pond to Long Pond to Round Pond and south to the Kunjamuk Road on International Paper Company land: This would occupy several days, especially if you add a trek to Long Pond Cliffs.

Kings Flow to Puffer Pond via the red trail, to Kings Flow again via the outlet path, to Wakely Brook, Humphrey Mountain, return to Round Pond, bushwhack around the pond and north on the Kunjamuk Road, walk down Big Brook Road to Kings Flow: a week-long loop through the woods.

References and Other Resources

References

Aber, Ted and Stella King. *The History of Hamilton County*. Lake Pleasant, NY: Great Wilderness Books, 1965. Quotes from pages 431, 438, 622, 927, 929, and 935 appear in the Overview and the introduction to Chapter III.

Hochschild, Harold F. *Life and Leisure in the Adirondacks*. Blue Mountain, NY: The Adirondack Museum, 1962. Quotes from pages 97–98 appear in the Overview, courtesy of the Adirondack Museum of the Adirondack Historical Association, who holds the copyright.

Krieger, Medora Hooper. *Geology of the Thirteenth Lake Quadrangle*. Albany, NY: New York State University Bulletin of the University of the State of New York, 1937. Background for the introduction to Chapter I and section 67.

McMartin, Barbara. *Discover the Southeastern Adirondacks: Old Roads and Open Peaks*. Woodstock, VT: Backcountry Publications, 1986.

McMartin, Barbara. *50 Hikes in the Adirondacks*. Woodstock, VT: Backcountry Publications, 1980.

Miller, William J. *The Great Rift on Chimney Mountain*. Albany, NY: Report to the Director, New York State Museum, 1914.

Rickett, Harold William. *Wild Flowers of the United States, Volume I, The Northeastern States*. New York: The New York Botanical Garden and McGraw-Hill Book Company, 1966.

Van Diver, Bradford G., Ph.D. *Rocks and Routes of the North Country New York*. Geneva, NY: W. F. Humphrey Press, Inc., 1976.

Wherry, Edgar T. *The Fern Guide, Northeastern and Midland United States and Adjacent Canada*. Philadelphia, PA: The Morris Arboretum of the University of Pennsylvania, 1972.

Other Resources

New York State Department of Environmental Conservation (DEC), 50
  Wolf Road, Albany, NY 12233
For plants:
  DEC List of Rare and Endangered Plants
For trails:
  DEC Brochure, *Nordic Skiing and Snowshoeing Trails*
  DEC Regional Office, Warrensburg, NY 12885
  DEC Regional Office, Northville, NY 12134
  DEC Indian Lake Islands Headquarters, Indian Lake, NY 12842
  Office of Tourism, Town of Lake Pleasant, Speculator, NY 12164
  Adirondack Mountain Club, RD3 Box 3055, Lake George, NY 12801

For other things to do in the Adirondacks:
  New York State Department of Commerce, Albany, NY 12245, "I Love
  New York" series: *Camping, Tourism Map, State Travel Guide.*

Index

Guidebooks from Backcountry Publications

State Parks and Campgrounds
State Parks and Campgrounds in Northern New York, $9.95

Walks and Rambles Series
Walks and Rambles on the Delmarva Peninsula, $8.95
Walks and Rambles in Dutchess and Putnam Counties (NY), $9.95
Walks and Rambles in Rhode Island, $9.95
Walks and Rambles in the Upper Connecticut River Valley, $9.95
Walks and Rambles in Westchester (NY) and Fairfield (CT) Counties, $8.95

Biking Series
25 Mountain Bike Tours in Vermont, $9.95
25 Bicycle Tours on Delmarva, $8.95
25 Bicycle Tours in Eastern Pennsylvania, $8.95
20 Bicycle Tours in the Finger Lakes, $8.95
20 Bicycle Tours in the Five Boroughs (NYC), $8.95
25 Bicycle Tours in the Hudson Valley, $9.95
25 Bicycle Tours in Maine, $9.95
25 Bicycle Tours in New Hampshire, $7.95
25 Bicycle Tours in New Jersey, $8.95
20 Bicycle Tours in and around New York City, $7.95
25 Bicycle Tours in Vermont, $8.95

Canoeing Series
Canoe Camping Vermont and New Hampshire Rivers, $7.95
Canoeing Central New York, $10.95
Canoeing Massachusetts, Rhode Island and Connecticut, $7.95

Hiking Series
50 Hikes in the Adirondacks, $11.95
50 Hikes in Central New York, $9.95
50 Hikes in Central Pennsylvania, $9.95
50 Hikes in Eastern Pennsylvania, $10.95
50 Hikes in the Hudson Valley, $10.95
50 Hikes in Massachusetts, $11.95
50 More Hikes in New Hampshire, $9.95
50 Hikes in New Jersey, $10.95
50 Hikes in Northern Maine, $10.95
50 Hikes in Ohio, $12.95
50 Hikes in Southern Maine, $10.95
50 Hikes in Vermont, $11.95
50 Hikes in West Virginia, $9.95
50 Hikes in Western New York, $12.95
50 Hikes in Western Pennsylvania, $11.95
50 Hikes in the White Mountains, $12.95

Ski-Touring Series
25 Ski Tours in Central New York, $7.95
25 Ski Tours in New Hampshire, $8.95
25 Ski Tours in Vermont, $8.95

The above titles are available at bookstores and at certain sporting goods stores or may be ordered directly from the publisher. For complete descriptions of these and other guides, write: The Countryman Press, P.Q. Box 175, Woodstock, VT 05091.